REPORT

TO THE

EXECUTIVE COMMITTEE OF
PUBLIC SERVICE CORPORATION OF NEW JERSEY

ON THE PROPOSED VEHICULAR TUNNEL
BETWEEN THE CITIES OF JERSEY CITY
AND NEW YORK

REPORT

TO THE

EXECUTIVE COMMITTEE OF
PUBLIC SERVICE CORPORATION OF NEW JERSEY

ON THE PROPOSED VEHICULAR TUNNEL
BETWEEN THE CITIES OF JERSEY CITY
AND NEW YORK BY THE SPECIAL
COMMITTEE APPOINTED TO INVESTIGATE
THE SUBJECT

PUBLISHED BY ORDER OF
THE BOARD OF DIRECTORS OF
PUBLIC SERVICE CORPORATION OF NEW JERSEY

MARCH, 1917

Transportation
Library
TF
238
H73
P98

REPORT ON

PROPOSED VEHICULAR TUNNEL

BETWEEN THE

CITIES OF JERSEY CITY AND NEW YORK

Report on the Proposed Vehicular Tunnel between the Cities of Jersey City and New York

To the Executive Committee of Public Service Corporation of New Jersey:

For many years the problem of providing better facilities for vehicular communication between New Jersey and New York has been under discussion, and with the growth of New Jersey, the need for a highway bridge or tunnel has each year become more apparent. The demand for better facilities and the suggestion that the construction of vehicular tunnels between the States would greatly benefit Public Service through the development of the territory served by it, was first called to your attention by the President in the month of November, 1913. The President on January 18th, 1916, in connection with a report on the subject made by Mr. Percy Ingalls, General Agent, again presented the subject for your consideration, stating that as ten years had elapsed, during which the project had been continuously discussed as a public enterprise, with no immediate prospect of its consummation, he would recommend that Public Service cause the whole subject to be thoroughly investigated with a view to determining the practicability of the construction of such a tunnel by Public Service.

As a result of this recommendation, the Executive Committee, on February 1st, 1916, passed a resolution appointing a special Committee to make a report on the feasibility and probable cost of such a tunnel, with authority to expend such sums as might be required to secure the necessary statistical and engineering information. This Committee consisted of the President, First Vice-President, Secretary, Engineer Maintenance of Way, Public Service Railway Company, and Mr. Walton Clark.

Your special Committee has made an investigation of the subject and begs to report as follows:

The construction of a vehicular tunnel under the waters of the Hudson River, in the judgment of your Committee, will be of inestimable benefit to the whole metropolitan district, and is essential to the proper industrial development of Northern New Jersey. Vehicular transportation by ferries is antiquated and inadequate for present day needs, to say nothing of the future. This is well illustrated by photographic exhibits annexed to this report, showing conditions that obtain at the entrance to the Cortlandt and Desbrosses Street ferries in Exchange Place, Jersey City. (See Exhibit No. 1.) The tremendous industrial development that has taken place in Brooklyn and Long Island City since the opening of the bridges over the East River affords a practical illustration of what might be expected in Northern New Jersey, where land is relatively cheap, if direct vehicular communication is provided. The lower portion of Jersey City and the entire Newark and Hackensack meadows district would immediately become readily accessible and available for warehouse and manufacturing purposes.

State Bridge and Tunnel Commissions:

As far back as the year 1906 the Legislatures of the States of New Jersey and New York, appreciating the importance of this subject, passed laws authorizing the appointment of State Commissions to study the subject of vehicular highways between States. These Commissions have ever since been continued, with the exception that between April 5th, 1911, and April 15th, 1912, no New Jersey Commission existed.

The personnel of the two Commissions at present is as follows:

The New Jersey Interstate Bridge and Tunnel Commission:
W. H. Noyes, Tenafly, N. J.
Colonel J. Hollis Wells, Jersey City, N. J.
DeWitt Van Buskirk, Bayonne, N. J.
George Limouze, Weehawken, N. J.
John J. O'Leary, Passaic, N. J.
   Thomas McMahon, Secretary.

The New York State Bridge and Tunnel Commission:
George R. Dyer, Chairman, 36 Wall St., New York City, N. Y.
E. W. Bloomingdale, 115 Broadway, New York City, N. Y.
A. J. Shamberg, 115 Broadway, New York City, N. Y.
McDougal Hawkes, 32 Nassau St., New York City, N. Y.
F. J. H. Kracke, Municipal Building, New York City, N. Y.
   Morris M. Frohlich, Secretary.

The Commissions have each had appropriations from time to time, which have been expended in engineering investigations of suggested sites for bridges and tunnels. The latest investigation resulted in a report from Messrs. Boller, Hodge and Baird, Consulting Engineers, submitted under date of February 24th, 1913, to the New Jersey Commission, and March 18th, 1913, to the New York Commission, stating that a bridge from about 57th Street, New York City, to the Hudson County Boulevard at Weehawken, N. J., was practicable, and this site most favorable, and that the cost would be approximately $42,000.000.

A report was also submitted by Messrs. Jacobs and Davies, builders of the Hudson and Manhattan, and Pennsylvania Tunnels, recommending the construction of a pair of tunnels between 12th Street, Jersey City, and Canal Street, New York City, at an estimated cost of $11,000,000.

The Constitution of the State of New Jersey prohibits the creation of a debt of more than $100,000 for such a public improvement, as a State enterprise, without the affirmative vote of the people of the State. To avoid this necessity, the New Jersey Legislature in 1914, passed the following Act, which was approved on April 17th, 1914 (Chapter 245, Laws of 1914):

BE IT ENACTED by the Senate and General Assembly of the State of New Jersey:

1. Three or more Counties of this State whose territory is contiguous, and one of which is partially bounded by a navigable stream or river, which stream or river is one of the boundaries of this State, may join together as provided in this act for the purpose of constructing and maintaining across such stream or river one or more bridges or tunnels, as may be suitable or necessary, to provide passage across or under such stream or river for traffic of all kinds.

2. When the consent and request of any three or more of such Counties expressed and declared as hereinafter provided is duly filed in the office of the Secretary of State, it shall be the duty of the Governor to appoint by and with the advice and consent of the Senate, three suitable persons from each of said Counties, and one person a resident of the State but not a resident of any of such Counties, who shall be known as The .... River Bridge and Tunnel Commission (inserting in the blank space the name of such stream or river) for a term of three years. Said commissioners shall have the power and it shall be their duty to procure and have made and prepared the necessary and proper plan or plans of such bridge or tunnel, to select the location of same and make the necessary estimates of the cost of construction of such bridge or tunnel; and when further authorized as herein set forth, the said Commission in conjunction with a similar body appointed by the City, State or County with which such bridge or tunnel will connect or with such city, State or county, shall have the power to enter into the necessary contract or contracts to build, equip and maintain the same. The consent and request of any county to the Governor to appoint such commission shall be by resolution duly passed at a regular meeting of the governing board of such counties after such notice and in such form as is required to duly obligate a county to enter into any legal contract for the payment of money; and shall authorize such commission to prepare such plans and specifications and procure estimates of the cost and maintenance of such bridge or tunnel; the cost to each of said counties to be fixed in such resolution not exceeding, however, a cost to each of said counties of the sum of ten thousand dollars, which said sum such counties shall agree to become responsible for and pay; provided, however, that in no event shall any county be bound by any action of its board of freeholders, unless and until, the board of freeholders, respectively, of two other counties, as aforesaid, shall have each also adopted the resolution calling for the appointment of the said bridge and tunnel commission; and provided, further, that if any board

of freeholders shall adopt such resolution as aforesaid, the same shall be and become ineffectual and void unless re-enacted, after a period of six months from its original adoption in the event that similar resolutions shall not in the meantime have been adopted by two other counties, as aforesaid.

3. As soon after such request and consent of any three counties for the appointment of a commission shall have been made to the Governor, as provided for herein, the Governor shall appoint such commissioners as herein provided, who shall proceed forthwith to prepare such plans and specifications and make such estimates, and for that purpose are authorized to employ the necessary engineers, counsel, clerks and other assistants as may be necessary, to have such plans and specifications prepared. Said commission shall be and become a body corporate, adopt a seal, and have power to sue and be sued. The commissioners provided to be appointed herein shall hold office for the time as herein provided and shall serve without remuneration. One of said commissioners from each of such counties shall be appointed for one year, one for two years and one for three years, and one commissioner from each of such counties shall be appointed annually thereafter. The person so appointed a commissioner, but who shall not reside in any of such counties, shall be appointed for a term of three years, and should the office of any commissioner become vacant for any reason, his successor shall be appointed for the unexpired term only.

4. After the preparation of such plans and specifications and estimate of cost, the said commission shall transmit the same duly certified to the governing bodies, respectively, of each county which has consented to the appointment of said commission, together with all the information and other data concerning the cost of construction and maintenance of such bridge or tunnel, which they have procured or have in their possession.

5. Thereafter, but not later than one year after the receipt by each of the said governing bodies of such plans, specifications and estimates, the governing bodies of such counties may, by proper resolution, request said commission to proceed with the construction of such bridge or tunnel; provided, however, that one-half of the total cost of the same, shall not exceed three per centum of the tax ratables of the real and personal property of such counties for the last preceding year, and upon receipt of such request in the form herein provided for from at least three of said counties, the said commission is hereby authorized and empowered to proceed with the construction of such bridge or tunnel in accordance with and subject to such limitations or restrictions as the governing bodies of such counties may prescribe, and is duly authorized to enter into the proper and necessary contract or contracts for the erection, equipment and operation of the same; such resolution shall be in such form and of such effect as to obligate each of the said counties for the amounts agreed to be paid by such counties in such resolution.

6. The method of providing for the payment of the cost and construction of said bridge or tunnel and the expense of operating or maintaining the same so far as said cost or expense shall be a charge upon the counties consenting to the appointment of said commission, shall be determined by the governing bodies of said county, in agreement with the said commission, and shall, by the terms of said agreement be distributed among said counties and borne by each of them in such proportion as may be set out in such agreement. From time to time as the building of such bridge or tunnel progresses said commission may require each of said counties to pay said commission its proportionate share of the cost of building and maintenance. Such counties are hereby authorized to issue bonds to provide the necessary money to make the payments required by said commission. Such bonds to be in such amounts and to bear interest not exceeding five per centum per annum, and shall be payable at such time and place as the governing bodies of such counties may, by resolution, fix and determine.

7. Such commissioners shall not be authorized or empowered to incur any expense or charge whatsoever for the construction of said bridge or tunnel except for the preliminary plans and surveys and estimate of cost, until the proper county or municipality with which said bridge or tunnel shall connect, shall be duly authorized and empowered and shall have duly entered into a binding obligation with said commission to pay one-half of the cost of such bridge or tunnel, and the repairs and maintenance of the same. In addition to the share of the cost of constructing such bridge or tunnel, the cost of maintenance and repairs of said bridge or tunnel, less such sums as may be received for the use of said bridge or tunnel from tolls or otherwise shall be paid each year by such counties to such commissioners.

8. Said commission is hereby also authorized subject to the restrictions contained in this act, and the restrictions imposed upon them by said counties, to enter into an agreement or agreements with a similar commission or body of such other State or municipality with which such bridge or tunnel shall connect or with such State, city, county or municipality for the joint maintenance and operation of the same, and to fix such tolls as may be just, reasonable and proper, and for the proper policing, lighting and keeping of such bridge or tunnel, and generally for the carrying out of the provisions of this act.

9. Said commission shall have full power in their own corporate name to purchase and acquire all lands, rights and interest in lands, either within or outside the territory of such counties, which may be necessary for the construction of such bridge or tunnel and for this purpose are authorized to condemn the same in the manner provided by the general laws of this State relating to the condemnation of lands for public use.

10. Whenever any work to be performed or material to be furnished shall involve an expenditure of any sum of money exceeding the sum

of two thousand dollars, the said commissioners shall designate the time when they will meet at their usual place of meeting to receive proposals in writing for doing the work and furnishing the material; and said commissioners shall order its clerk to give notice by advertisement, inserted in at least two newspapers printed and circulating respectively in each of such counties, at least ten days before the time of such meeting, of the work to be done and materials to be furnished, of which at the time of such order they shall cause to be filed in their office particular specifications.

All proposals received shall be publicly opened by the said commissioners and the commissioners shall award the contract to the lowest responsible bidder; all contractors shall be required to give bond satisfactory in amount and security to the said commissioners.

11. Notwithstanding the agreement and consent of any three or more counties, as aforesaid, the said commission shall not be authorized to take any proceedings or incur any expense or obligation whatever until the terms and conditions of said agreement and consent shall have been reviewed and approved by three Justices of the Supreme Court, especially designated by the Governor for that purpose. Said Justices shall designate a time and place for the holding of a public hearing on the question of the approval of the terms of said agreement, at which said hearing all persons interested may be heard. If said agreement shall be approved and confirmed by the said three Justices, then the same shall be in all respects binding upon the counties so consenting to said agreement; except that in no event shall the obligation to be assumed or imposed upon any county for the construction of any bridges or tunnels exceed ten millions of dollars.

12. This act shall take effect immediately.

Approved April 17, 1914.

Pursuant to this Act, the County of Bergen on August 3rd, 1914, passed a resolution requesting the appointment of Commissioners and appropriating $10,000 for expenses. The County of Hudson passed a similar resolution on April 5th, 1915, but because of the provision in the Act that at least three Counties must adopt similar resolutions within a period of six months, and as none of the other Counties had acted, these resolutions became inoperative, and on November 11th, 1915 the County of Hudson and on November 22nd, 1915 the County of Bergen, again passed resolutions. The limit of time having once more expired, Hudson County passed a resolution on February 14th, 1917, and it is understood that Bergen County will again act whenever a third County is ready to request the appointment of a Commission. The Boards of Freeholders of Passaic and Union Counties have shown no disposition to join in this investigation, and the Board of Chosen Freeholders of the County of Essex, while it has held special hearings on the subject, has taken no formal action. At a recent meeting, however, the Board of Chosen Freeholders of Essex County, influenced by agitation in favor of a tunnel by various commercial bodies, and the attention which has been given the project by the Governor of New Jersey, and the press, committed itself to take favorable action in May, 1917 when its financial budget will permit of the necessary appropriation.

As the Act of 1914 requires the advice and consent of the New Jersey State Senate, in connection with the appointment of Commissioners by the Governor of the State, it is apparent that the deferring of action by the Board of Chosen Freeholders of the County of Essex until May, 1917 will result in delaying the appointment of Commissioners until 1918 unless the Governor of the State calls a special session of the State Senate.

No effort has been made to obtain legislation in New York State, it being the opinion of the New York Commissioners that prompt action by the Legislature of the State of New York, and by the City of New York, will follow the agreement of three Counties in New Jersey.

Vehicular Traffic over Ferries Between New Jersey and New York:

A number of traffic counts have been made by your Committee, and previously, of vehicles crossing Hudson River ferries at different seasons of the year, to obtain information as to the flow of traffic, hour of greatest traffic, and general characteristics of traffic over the ferries. The information furnished by the railroads, upon request, not being in sufficient detail for a careful estimate of the amount of traffic which would use a tunnel if constructed.

The first and most complete count was made during June and July, 1913, covering two week days and one Sunday (24 hours), and all ferries from the Central Railroad Company ferry at Communipaw to the Public Service Ferry at Edgewater. The record obtained, with detail of traffic by hours, is attached hereto as Exhibit No. 2. The count showed, on the assumption that the two week days gave a fair average for 300 working days, and that the count made on Sunday gave a fair average for 65 Sundays and holidays, that the traffic in 1913 over all ferries from Edgewater to the Central Railroad Company ferry at Communipaw, amounted to 6,130,945 vehicles, and returned a revenue of $1,700,658, at an average rate of 27¾c per vehicle.

On December 29th, 1915 a further twenty-four hour count was made of vehicles crossing Cortlandt Street, Desbrosses Street and Chambers Street ferries. This count was of little value as it showed a falling off in the amount of traffic, and it developed that this was caused by the holiday season, when business was known to be sub-normal.

After considering the traffic over each ferry, your Committee determined that a tunnel in the vicinity of 12th Street, Jersey City, and Canal Street, New York City, the location suggested by Messrs. Jacobs and Davies, would be favorably located to serve the heavy vehicular traffic now using Cortlandt Street, Barclay Street, Chambers Street, Desbrosses Street and Christopher Street ferries. These ferries are hereinafter referred to as "the five ferries".

On the 18th and 19th days of December, 1916, a count was made of the traffic over "the five ferries" during the hours between 8 A. M. and 12 o'clock noon, and between 1 P. M. and 7 P. M. The record obtained is hereto attached as Exhibit No. 3.

A comparison of the ten-hour count, made in December, 1916, with the same hours recorded in June and July, 1913, showed a percentage of change in the number of vehicles passing over "the five ferries", as follows:

Cortlandt Street	22.34% increase
Barclay Street	6.99% decrease
Chambers Street	24.92% decrease
Desbrosses Street	49.54% increase
Christopher Street	1.87% decrease
Total for five ferries, 3½ yrs	11.91% increase

A comparison of a traffic count made in June and July, 1913, with a traffic count made in December, 1916, is not, in the opinion of your Committee, accurately indicative of the growth. The Hoboken ferries, for example, in 1916 had lost all of the traffic going to the Hamburg-American and North German Lloyd Piers in 1913. The Chambers Street ferry in the summer time carries large quantities of fresh vegetables and fruit to the New York Market, and this traffic is lacking in December. It is the belief of your Committee that under normal conditions vehicular traffic between New Jersey and New York is increasing, and will increase at the rate of at least 5% per year with the facilities for communication offered by ferries, and that the opening of a tunnel will considerably increase this percentage of growth.

Probable Effect of a Vehicular Tunnel on the Present Lighterage System:

Your Committee believes that the New Jersey railroads would welcome any method by which New York City freight would be received and delivered in New Jersey, but existing freight rates are such as to make it unlikely that a tunnel would induce shippers to truck across the river. Each railroad maintains a number of freight docks on the Manhattan water front within the lighterage limits (136th Street on the north, Bay Ridge on the south and 154th Street on the East River), and to each of these docks, the freight rate, from points distant approximately fifty miles or more, is the same as the rate to the New Jersey terminals. The freight stations on Manhattan Island are so located as to reduce trucking to a minimum, and an inducement in the shape of lower New Jersey freight rates must be offered before much freight would be trucked to and from the New Jersey railroad terminals. Commercial organizations in New Jersey are now making a determined effort to overcome the existing inequitable discrimination against New Jersey in forcing payment of lighterage charges on freight not lightered, and the case is now before the Interstate Commerce Commission. Should this effort result in reduced freight rates within New Jersey, a considerable saving could be made by trucking to and from the New Jersey terminals, and the use of a vehicular tunnel would increase accordingly.

For the purpose of this report, however, your Committee has considered only the probable diversion to a tunnel of a portion of the existing vehicular traffic across the river, the normal growth of same, and the influence of the tunnel on the development of the territory.

Ferry Rates for Vehicles:

Owing to differences in classification, it is difficult to prepare comparative tables of rates for the several ferries. The following is taken from the Pennsylvania Railroad Company schedule:

Vehicle	Horses	Description	Rate
Carriage	1 horse,	not exceeding 2 persons	13c
"	2 "	" " 3 "	25c
"	2 "	" " 5 "	30c
Business wagon	1 "	with or without load	13c
" "	2 "	" " " "	25c
Beer "	2 "	" " " "	38c
Trucks	2 "	loaded	50c
Coal Wagons	2 "	"	38c
Pleasure Auto			25c to 75c
Auto Trucks			40c to 70c
Business Auto			25c

A careful examination of these rates leads your Committee to believe that the average fare of 27.75 cents, reported for all classes of vehicles over all ferries in 1913, is considerably lower than the average fare paid by the class of vehicles which would patronize a tunnel.

Tunnel Tolls for Vehicles:

Your Committee believes that motor-driven vehicles will use a conveniently located tunnel in preference to a ferry at the same rates of fare. For the purpose of this report, therefore, we suggest as tunnel rates the Pennsylvania Railroad ferry rates quoted above, believing that the class of vehicles using a tunnel will pay, at these rates, an average fare of 35 cents per trip.

Percentage of Motor Vehicles to Total Vehicles:

In making counts of traffic, a separate record was kept of the number of motor vehicles, it being believed that a vehicular tunnel under the Hudson River would attract motor vehicles because of a saving in time, but that it would not attract slow moving vehicles because of a loss, in both time and energy. The increased use of motor vehicles is, therefore, of great interest in considering the probable tunnel traffic. The following table shows the increase during the past three years over "the five ferries":

PERCENTAGE OF MOTOR VEHICLES TO TOTAL VEHICLES

	1913	1915	1916
Cortlandt St.—P. R. R.	11.29%	17.8%	24.11%
Barclay St.—D. L. & W. R. R.	6.5 %		16.13%
Chambers St.—Erie R. R.	3.64%	14.7%	14.07%
Desbrosses St.—P. R. R.	12.43%	22.7%	30.93%
Christopher St.—D. L. & W. R. R.	8.64%		17.50%

Figures obtained from the Department of Bridges of New York City show that in 1914, 49.4% of the total vehicles crossing the East River Bridges were motor-driven, and that in 1915 the number had increased to 57.6% and in 1916 to 67% of the total. A comparison of these percentages with similar percentages for the Hudson River ferries, given above, indicates that the exchange of horses for motors everywhere taking place has been greatly accelerated by the free bridges. Your Committee feels that these figures may be taken as indicative of the effect the opening of a tunnel would have on the traffic on the New Jersey side, although in the following estimate of tunnel traffic for the first year, only normal growth has been included.

Estimated Vehicular Traffic Through Proposed Tunnel:

To determine the points between which the heaviest flow of traffic occurs, the drivers of horse and motor trucks crossing "the five ferries", in both directions, were interviewed during the month of March, 1916, and information obtained as to the starting and destination points of each vehicle. One ton was adopted as a unit, and the movement of traffic recorded in units. A record was thus obtained of the movement of 8,146 units. Nine zones were laid out on each side of the river, as shown on Exhibit No. 4, and movements plotted to show the traffic between zones, with the ferries used. This resulted in a total of 405 possible zone-ferry combinations. As the traffic in many of these combinations was small, those showing traffic of less than fifty units were eliminated, reducing the total units reported to 7,089 in forty-eight zone-ferry combinations. This record gives a very fair indication of the routing of traffic between points in New Jersey and points in New York, although the traffic from and to Newark is at this time largely confined to the Lincoln Highway, formerly known as the Plank Road, because of the condition of the Turnpike, and, consequently, the selection of a ferry by this traffic is not the same as it would be normally.

The distances from the center of each zone to each ferry, and to the proposed tunnel entrances, were scaled, and to determine whether traffic would save time by using the proposed tunnel in place of existing ferries, experimental runs with a two-ton truck were made from the center of each zone, on each side of the river, to each ferry, and to the proposed tunnel entrances, and the time consumed recorded. In calculating the time by ferry, the actual time of operating from the zone center to the ferry was taken, plus one-half of the ferry headway to allow for time lost in waiting for a boat, plus the actual time of crossing, and plus the actual time required to reach the center of the zone on the opposite shore. It should be noted that the time of crossing by ferry herein recorded does not include the delays incident to the congested hours when vehicles have to wait for several boats (see Exhibit No. 1), nor the delays occurring because of fog, ice, or other river conditions affecting the headway of boats.

In calculating the time by the tunnel, the actual time of operating from the zone center to the tunnel entrance was taken, plus the time in the tunnel, at an estimated speed of ten miles per hour, plus the time of reaching the zone center on the opposite shore. All these records are attached hereto as Exhibit No. 5.

Data was collected on the cost of operating motor-driven trucks of varying sizes, and the cost of operating an average vehicle was determined by taking trucks of 1, 2, 3, 5, 7 and 10 ton capacity, using only variable items of operation, including depreciation, gasoline at 17c per gallon, oil, tires and repairs. This data is also shown in Exhibit No. 5.

This investigation showed an average saving in time for the 7,089 units recorded of 8.4 minutes for each river crossing by tunnel, at an increased cost of operating, chiefly due to the added tunnel distance, of 5.18 cents. As stated above, the calculation as to time distinctly favors the ferries by not taking into account the delays, so thoroughly understood, which are always incident to ferry service. The value of the time saved to an average vehicle is difficult to calculate. On the basis of a three ton truck, valued at $10.00 per day, and of a driver working eight hours for $4.00 per day, a saving of 8.4 minutes per trip, or 16.8 minutes per round trip, amounts to a saving of 3.5% of the truck and driver's day, or 49 cents. From this must be deducted the cost of operating a three ton truck the greater distance by tunnel at 5.18c per unit, per trip, or 31.08 cents for a three ton truck round trip, making a net saving on one round trip of 17.92 cents. A three ton truck, making four round trips per day, would save 71.68 cents per day. We have no knowledge of the average number of trips per truck, per day, and perhaps the main value of these figures is to show that crossing by tunnel would certainly be cheaper than crossing by ferry, even under the best ferry conditions.

The Pennsylvania and Erie Railroad Companies furnish the following figures showing vehicular traffic over ferries operated by them for the year 1916. This traffic, if increased at the rate of 5% per year, would, in 1920, the first year the tunnel could be operated if construction commenced in 1917, result in traffic as shown below:

	Total Vehicles 1916 Reported By Companies	Total Vehicles 1920 Estimated
Cortlandt St. Ferry	773,853	940,624
Desbrosses St. "	854,837	1,039,060
Chambers St. "	395,431	480,650
Total	2,024,121	2,460,334

The D. L. & W. Railroad Company keep no record of vehicles, but on the basis of the count made in 1913, increased at the rate of 5% per year, the traffic over its ferries in 1920 would be as follows:

	Total Vehicles 1913 Based on Count	Total Vehicles 1920 Estimated
Barclay Street Ferry	648,930	913,110
Christopher " "	444,300	625,176
Total	1,093,230	1,538,286

The total estimated number of vehicles crossing in the vicinity of "the five ferries" in 1920 is 3,998,620. Your Committee believes that more than 60% will be motor-driven, and that at least 2,000,000 vehicles will use a tunnel if existent in 1920 in the location named.

Vehicular Tunnels Under the River Thames, London, England:

Inasmuch as highway tunnels have been operated for many years under the River Thames in England, it was decided to investigate the conditions under which they operate. Accordingly, Mr. Percy Ingalls, Secretary of the Corporation, and Mr. H. C. Donecker, Assistant General Manager, Public Service Railway Company, went to England in August, 1916, and made a study of the Blackwall and Rotherhithe Tunnels under the River Thames. These tunnels are 6,200 and 6,826 feet long, respectively. A copy of the report on these tunnels is attached hereto as Exhibit No. 6. The report shows that a narrow tunnel roadway, properly policed, can accommodate two lines of vehicles moving in opposite directions, and permit the passing of vehicles going in the same direction, and that a speed can be maintained exceeding the speed maintained on a street of much greater width, for the reason that the flow of traffic is continuously in the same directions, with no vehicles leaving or joining the lines of traffic, no cross traffic, and no pedestrians. The report also shows that while each of these tunnels is used by approximately 2,000 vehicles per day, between the hours of 6 A. M. and 7 P. M., about 800 of which are motor-driven, and that the air is much vitiated, no prostrations from motor gases have ever been reported, notwithstanding that no artificial ventilation has been provided.

Method of Construction, Feasibility and Estimated Cost of the Proposed Vehicular Tunnel Under the Hudson River:

In order to determine the best and cheapest form of construction, and the feasibility of the project, your Committee, after a careful investigation of their qualifications for the work, retained three eminent engineers, Prof. William H. Burr, of New York, Chairman, Mr. Daniel E. Moran, of New York, and

Mr. Ralph Modjeski, of Chicago and New York, each of whom has had a wide experience in engineering and construction work, to act as a Board and make a report, including preliminary plans and estimates.

These gentlemen, under date of January 30th, 1917, submitted a unanimous report, a copy of which is attached hereto as Exhibit No. 7. This report recommends the construction of a tunnel by the following general methods, as indicated on Plate No. 2: Commencing on the New Jersey side, the land section to be constructed by the open cut method where the right-of-way is owned, and by the cut and cover method, similar to parts of the subway construction in New York City, where only a sub-surface easement is acquired. For the section between the New Jersey bulkhead and pierhead lines, by the open caisson, or by the pneumatic caisson method, as shown on Plates Nos. 11 and 12. For the river section, by a method quite similar to that employed in the construction of the original subway tunnel under the Harlem River and in the Detroit River Tunnel. This method requires the dredging of a trench in the bottom of the river to the required grade, and the driving of piles in this trench to provide a firm foundation. The tunnel for this portion to be built in sections of suitable length afloat, or on launching ways, at some convenient location, floated to the tunnel location, and sunk into place in the bed of the trench. The portion of the tunnel from a point about 600 feet outside of the New York pierhead line to the New York bulkhead line, as on the New Jersey side, to be constructed by the open caisson or by the pneumatic caisson method, as shown on Plates Nos. 11 and 12. For the land section on the New York side, by the usual cut and cover method. A variation from the method recommended for the river section is necessary where the tunnel approaches the shores to avoid damage to pier foundations, and because of rock found near the bed of the river on the New York side. While the method of construction varies and the river portion is consequently of different cross section from the other portions, the interior dimensions will be the same throughout.

The top of the tunnel structure is designed to be not less than fifty feet below mean low water, which depth was determined by the New York Harbor Board of Engineer Officers of the Army as the minimum depth which would be permitted. This decision was reached upon an application made in September, 1916, at the request of your Committee, by the New Jersey Interstate Bridge and Tunnel Commission to the Secretary of War. The tunnel recommended by the Board is 10,309 feet long from street entrance to street entrance, 9,409 feet long from portal to portal and 5,495 feet long from bulkhead to bulkhead. It has an interior space available for traffic 26 feet wide by 13 feet high. The roadway is 17 feet wide between curbs, with a 5½ ft. sidewalk on one side and a 3½ ft. standing space on the other side, as shown on Plate No. 4. The maximum grades on the two approaches are 3.85% for the Canal Street approach and 4.55% for the 12th Street approach in Jersey City, both being for short distances only, the prevailing grades being 3.16% and 2.21%, respectively.

The practicability of the method of ventilating the proposed tunnel, described in the Board's report, was confirmed by a series of experiments made on the property of the Company at Passaic Wharf, Newark, N. J. Your Committee caused to be constructed an air-tight building, one hundred and twenty-five feet long, as a model of a section of the proposed tunnel, with roadway, sidewalks, etc., complete, including air ducts with openings into the top and bottom of the tunnel, and electrically operated blowers and exhaust fans of proportionate size. The tunnel section was filled with gasoline motor trucks and automobiles of various sizes, to the number of eight in all, and a series of tests were made under the direction of Dr. Gellert Alleman, of Swarthmore College. Samples of air taken at many points in the tunnel, with all the cars running, throttled down and racing, with and without ventilation, were analyzed. Tests were made with fresh air introduced at the top and exhausted at the bottom and similar tests with the direction of the air reversed. The volume and velocity of the air so introduced was measured. The chemical analysis of the air samples taken during these tests, as reported by Dr. Alleman, is included herein as Appendix No. 10.

These tests prove that the general method of ventilation outlined by the Board is entirely feasible, and that the products of gasoline combustion and smoke can be overcome by the introduction of air in the quantities specified and exhausted as described, leaving the air practically normal. The model tunnel will be maintained in its present location, where it is available for inspection and demonstration.

In their report, the Board of Engineers say that it is entirely feasible to construct a vehicular tunnel under the Hudson River, between Canal Street, New York City, and Twelfth Street, Jersey City, with the top surface of the tube fifty feet below mean low water, and supported upon an adequate pile foundation on the line indicated in the plans attached to this report. That it is entirely feasible to ventilate satisfactorily such a tunnel tube when used by gasoline motor vehicles in numbers practically equal to its capacity. That the total estimated cost of construction of such a tunnel, fully equipped, is $6,899,000, at normal prices for labor and material, and $2,000,000 more, or $8,899,000 at prices now ruling, including contractors' profit, engineering and contingencies, but not including easements and real estate for entrances.

Your Committee after receiving the Board of Engineers' report submitted the proposed plan of construction to one of the largest contractors in New York City, and obtained a bid on the construction of the tunnel by the methods outlined. This bid was very close to the estimate of cost at present prices submitted by the Board, and in the opinion of your Committee, it positively confirms the Board's estimate.

The Board's report provides for a tunnel entrance in the block bounded by Grove, 13th, Henderson and 12th Streets, Jersey City, and the Board believes that it will be necessary to purchase this entire block. To reach this point, it will also be necessary to obtain an easement under property of either the D. L. & W. Railroad Company, or Erie Railroad Company, and your Committee estimates that the cost of land and easements on the New Jersey side may amount to $350,000.

On the New York side an easement will be required under dock property belonging to New York City, necessitating, during construction, the temporary abandonment of one slip, and easements under city streets to one of three entrances suggested by the Board, viz.: Canal Street, Spring Street or West Street. An entrance on either Canal Street or Spring Street would necessitate the purchase of property, either for street widening, or for entrance purposes. While the actual location of a tunnel entrance is indefinite, your Committee estimates that the cost of land and easements on the New York side may amount to $700,000.

The land purchased for tunnel entrances would be available after the completion of the tunnel for the construction of buildings. It is the belief of your Committee that use would be found for this land which would return sufficient income to pay taxes and interest on its cost.

Estimated Total Cost of Proposed Tunnel at Normal Prices for Labor and Material:

Public Service Investigation (expended)	$ 75,000
Board of Engineers' Construction Estimate	6,899,000
Land and Easements—New Jersey side	350,000
" " " —New York side	700,000
Interest during construction	425,000
Taxes during construction	80,000
Total cost	$8,529,000

Your Committee has assumed that for Public Service to finance the construction of a tunnel on the above estimate of cost, it will be necessary, following the general plan adopted in financing of Public Service Terminal, to form a Tunnel Company, having a paid-in capital stock of $1,000,000, to be owned by Public Service, the tunnel company to issue in addition, $9,000,000 of fifty year, 5% bonds, which can be sold at 85, netting $7,650,000, thus giving the tunnel company, after paying construction costs, a working capital of $121,000. To make these bonds salable, it will be necessary that Public Service guarantee both principal and interest. A forty-five year sinking fund of $42,300 per year, earning interest at 6% per annum, established after five years, would retire bonds at maturity.

Your Committee has assumed that a tunnel would pay an annual tax on property in Jersey City and New York equal to 2% of the cost of the tunnel, and in addition, a franchise tax on its gross receipts of 1% the first year, increasing at the rate of 1% annually until the tax reached 5% in the fifth year of operation.

Estimated First Year Earnings of Proposed Tunnel if Constructed at Normal Prices:

GROSS EARNINGS:		
2,000,000 vehicles per annum @ 35c		$700,000
OPERATING EXPENSES:		
Superintendence and Labor	$ 50,000	
Light and Power	50,000	
Repairs and Supplies	30,000	
Total Operating Expense		130,000
Profit from Operation before paying taxes and interest		570,000
TAXES:		
Taxes on $8,000,000 property @ 2%	$160,000	
Franchise Tax on $700,000 income @ 1%	7,000	
Total Taxes		167,000
NET PROFIT FROM OPERATION		403,000
Interest $9,000,000 bonds @ 5%		450,000
LOSS FROM FIRST YEAR'S OPERATION		$ 47,000

No return on $1,000,000 capital stock.

If the land at the tunnel entrances could be utilized so as to pay taxes and interest, amounting to $71,000, on its cost, the first year's operation would show a net profit of $24,000, or 2.4% on the capital stock of the tunnel company.

The estimated 2,000,000 vehicles passing through the tunnel in the first year of operation is based on the expected diversion to the tunnel of one-half of the total traffic of "the five ferries" in the year 1920. We believe that the normal increase in ferry traffic is about five per cent. per annum. We believe that the existence of the tunnel will stimulate river crossing traffic beyond the normal and that the traffic resulting from this stimulation will pass through the tunnel. We also believe that the facilities offered by the tunnel will encourage the already rapid substitution of motors for horses, thereby increasing the percentage of the total river crossing traffic which will use the tunnel. It is the belief of your Committee that after the first year of operation, the tunnel traffic will increase not less than ten per cent. per annum for at least the following five years.

Your Committee calls attention to the fact that the capacity of the tunnel to handle motor-driven vehicles is several times greater than the 2,000,000 vehicles per annum estimated, depending upon the speed of operation (see Exhibit No. 8), and that there will be no substantial increase in the expense of operating the tunnel if filled to capacity. An increase of 10% per annum in the number of vehicles using the tunnel would result as follows:

Estimated Earnings of Proposed Tunnel for First Six Years, if Constructed at Estimated Normal Prices for Labor and Material:

	No. of Vehicles	Gross Revenue	Total Operating Expenses, Including Taxes and Interest	Profit. No Return from Real Estate	Percentage of Return on Capital Invested	Profit. Real Estate Carrying its Taxes and Interest
1st Year	2,000,000	$ 700,000	$747,000	$ 47,000 Loss		$ 24,000
2nd "	2,200,000	770,000	755,400	14,600	1.4%	85,600
3rd "	2,420,000	847,000	765,410	81,590	8.1%	125,590
4th "	2,662,000	931,700	777,268	154,432	15.4%	225,432
5th "	2,928,200	1,024,870	791,243	233,627	23.3%	304,627
6th "	3,221,020	1,127,357	838,668	288,689	28.8%	359,689

Note—A sinking fund charge of $42,300 is included in expenses for the sixth year.

Estimated Total Cost of Proposed Tunnel at the Present Abnormal Prices for Labor and Material:

Public Service Investigation (expended)	$ 75,000
Board of Engineers' Construction Estimate	8,899,000
Land and Easements—New Jersey side	350,000
" " " New York side	700,000
Interest during construction	500,000
Taxes during construction	94,000
Total cost	$10,618,000

Your Committee again assumes the incorporation of a tunnel company by Public Service, having a paid-in capital of $1,000,000. The tunnel company to issue $11,500,000 of fifty year, 5% bonds, guaranteed by Public Service, to be sold at 85, netting $9,775,000, thus giving a working capital of $157,000 after paying construction costs. A forty-five year sinking fund amounting to $54,050 per annum, established after five years, would retire bonds at maturity.

Your Committee has again assumed a 2% property tax on the cost of the tunnel and a franchise tax on gross earnings increasing from 1% for the first year, to 5% for the fifth year.

Estimated First Year Earnings of Proposed Tunnel, if Constructed at the Present Abnormal Prices:

GROSS EARNINGS:
    2,000,000 vehicles per annum @ 35c $700,000

OPERATING EXPENSES:
    Superintendence and Labor $50,000
    Light and Power 50,000
    Repairs and Supplies 30,000

        Total Operating Expense 130,000

    Profit from operation before paying taxes & interest 570,000

TAXES:
    Taxes on $10,000,000 property @ 2% $200,000
    Franchise Tax on $700,000 income @ 1% 7,000

        Total Taxes 207,000

NET PROFIT FROM OPERATION $363,000
Interest on $11,500,000 bonds @ 5% 575,000

LOSS FROM FIRST YEAR'S OPERATION $212,000

As in the former estimate, the loss for the first year of operation would be reduced by $71,000 to $141,000, if land included for entrances is utilized in such a way as to earn sufficient to pay taxes and interest on its cost.

Estimated Earnings of Proposed Tunnel for First Six Years, if Constructed at Present Abnormal Prices for Labor and Material:

	No. of Vehicles	Gross Revenue	Total Operating Expenses, Including Taxes and Interest	Profit. No Return from Real Estate	Percentage of Return on Capital Invested	Profit. Real Estate Carrying its Taxes and Interest	
1st Year	2,000,000	$ 700,000	$912,000	$212,000 Loss		$141,000	Loss
2nd "	2,200,000	770,000	920,400	150,400 "		79,400	"
3rd "	2,420,000	847,000	930,410	83,410 "		12,410	"
4th "	2,662,000	931,700	942,268	10,568 "		60,432	
5th "	2,928,200	1,024,870	956,243	68,627	6.8%	139,627	
6th "	3,221,020	1,127,357	1,015,418	111,939	11.1%	182,939	

Note—A sinking fund charge of $54.050 is included in expenses for the sixth year.

Proposed Tunnel as a State or Municipal Project:

Your Committee in its investigation has covered much of the ground and obtained perhaps all of the information, except detailed plans and specifications, and actual competitive bids on construction, which would have resulted from an investigation if instituted by New York and the several Counties of New Jersey under the authority given the Counties by the Legislative Act of 1914. The information collected, if placed at the disposal of the interested Counties, would advance the project to a point where its consummation or rejection as a public enterprise can be quickly determined. There can be no doubt from the standpoint of industrial development as to the desirability of a tunnel operated as a free public highway, as against private operation with tolls approximating ferry charges. The cost of construction in either case would be substantially the same and the following tables show the estimated cost of public operation.

Estimated Cost of Operating Proposed Tunnel under Public Ownership if built at Normal Prices for Labor and Material:

Operating Expenses—
    Superintendence and Labor $50,000
    Light and Power 50,000
    Repairs and Supplies 30,000 $130,000

No Taxes
Interest on $8,500,000 bonds @ 4%.................................. 340,000

    Total Annual Cost..$470,000

Estimated Cost of Operating Proposed Tunnel under Public Ownership, if built at Present Abnormal Prices for Labor and Material:

Operating Expenses—
    Superintendence and Labor $50,000
    Light and Power 50,000
    Repairs and Supplies 30,000 $130,000

No Taxes
Interest on $10,500,000 bonds @ 4%................................ 420,000

    Total Annual Cost..$550,000

Operating expenses given above are the same as estimated under private operation, although it is quite certain that the cost of superintendence, labor and supplies would increase under public operation.

From the foregoing, it is apparent that if the tunnel is to be constructed and operated as a free public highway by Governmental agencies, it will entail a total annual Governmental burden of approximately one-half million dollars.

Conclusion:

The tunnel contemplated by this report is for vehicular purposes only. It is not thought that a single roadway, ample in itself for vehicular traffic in both directions, should be complicated by rail traffic. Existing facilities, with proper additions thereto, can doubtless be made to take care of passenger transportation. In all events, the subject matter of this report deals with an entirely different problem.

Your Committee believes that the thing of prime importance is the early construction of the tunnel, that the question of by whom it should be constructed is of lesser importance, except that the benefit derived therefrom would be greater if it were operated as a free highway than if tolls were charged. Obviously it is out of the question for it to be constructed as a free public highway by private capital. Your Committee, therefore, now recommends that this report be made public, in the hope that it will result in the early construction of the tunnel as a free public highway. In default of such construction by governmental agencies, and upon the return of costs of construction to approximately the standards of the Spring of 1914, herein referred to as "normal prices", your Committee will bring the matter again to your attention with a further recommendation. In the meantime, the growth and course of over-river motor traffic will be watched and studied.

There has been expended by your Committee, under the authority given it, in and about the preparation of this report, the reports and exhibits annexed thereto, the approximate sum of $75,000.

Your Committee desires to express thanks to the members of the New Jersey Interstate Bridge and Tunnel Commission, the officers of the various railroads terminating in New Jersey, Messrs. Jacobs and Davies, of New York, Sir Albert H. Stanley, of London, Mr. G. W. Humphreys, Chief Engineer, London City Council, and Messrs. Humphreys and Glasgow, of London, for the assistance rendered by them.

Respectfully submitted,

THOS. N. MCCARTER,
GEO. J. ROBERTS,
PERCY INGALLS,
MARTIN SCHREIBER,
WALTON CLARK.

February 20th, 1917.

EXHIBIT 1.

PENNSYLVANIA RAILROAD FERRIES

JERSEY CITY

BECAUSE OF CONGESTION

VEHICLES WAIT FOR SEVERAL BOATS

MONTGOMERY AND GREENE STREETS, JERSEY CITY, N. J.
General view looking east toward Exchange Place, showing trucks lined up from ferry entrance to the east side of Greene Street on Montgomery Street.
Taken December 21st, 1916, at 10 A. M.

MONTGOMERY AND GREENE STREETS, JERSEY CITY, N. J.
General view looking east toward Exchange Place, showing trucks lined up from ferry entrance to the east side of Greene Street on Montgomery Street.
Taken January 4th, 1917, at 12:00 M.

MONTGOMERY AND GREENE STREETS, JERSEY CITY, N. J.
General view looking east toward Exchange Place, showing trucks lined up from ferry entrance to the east side of Greene Street on Montgomery Street.

Taken January 4th, 1917, at 12:30 P. M.

EXHIBIT 2.

TWENTY-FOUR HOUR RECORD OF VEHICULAR

TRAFFIC CROSSING THE HUDSON RIVER

ON ALL FERRIES BETWEEN

NEW JERSEY AND NEW YORK CITY.

TAKEN DURING MONTHS OF JUNE AND JULY, 1913,

ON TWO WEEK DAYS AND ONE SUNDAY.

	Boats	Vehicles	Fares	Average Fare
LIBERTY STREET—Central R. R. of N. J.				
First week-day	257	1390	$433.58	.3119
Second week-day	261	1602	490.83	.3064
Sunday	214	216	52.28	.2420
CORTLANDT STREET—P. R. R.				
First week-day	240	2045	525.04	.2567
Second week-day	241	1938	490.76	.2635
Sunday	167	810	260.16	.3213
CORTLANDT STREET—W. S. R. R.				
First week-day	139	848	253.60	.2991
Second week-day	140	855	249.19	.2915
Sunday	102	346	115.95	.3351
BARCLAY STREET—D., L. & W. R. R.				
First week-day	241	2185	520.50	.2382
Second week-day	241	1967	452.39	.2300
Sunday	157	402	105.77	.2631
CHAMBERS STREET—Erie R. R.				
First week-day	212	1674	447.78	.2675
Second week-day	210	1609	435.73	.2708
Sunday	163	396	130.19	.3288
DESBROSSES STREET—P. R. R.				
First week-day	267	2589	766.51	.2961
Second week-day	261	2549	771.70	.3027
Sunday	166	487	153.52	.3152
CHRISTOPHER STREET—D. L., & W. R. R.				
First week-day	214	1359	313.93	.2310
Second week-day	215	1512	349.70	.2313
Sunday	159	210	53.80	.2562
23rd STREET—Central R. R. of N. J.				
First week-day	106	904	292.33	.3234
Second week-day	109	913	296.89	.3252
Sunday	97	100	28.61	.2861
23rd STREET—D., L. & W. R. R.				
First week-day	194	1112	287.21	.2583
Second week-day	200	1027	273.29	.2661
Sunday	155	225	55.26	.2456
23rd STREET—Erie R. R.				
First week-day	118	1239	323.26	.2609
Second week-day	119	1206	316.37	.2623
Sunday	76	169	53.27	.3152
14th and 23rd STREETS—Hoboken				
First week-day	226	1307	316.12	.2419
Second week-day	224	1432	345.30	.2411
Sunday	180	413	124.88	.3024

	Boats	Vehicles	Fares	Average Fare
42ND STREET—W. S. R. R., WEEHAWKEN				
First week-day	193	1404	453.91	.3233
Second week-day	204	1456	467.32	.3210
Sunday	199	1508	468.77	.3109
42ND STREET—W. S. R. R., W. N. Y.				
First week-day	82	416	124.63	.2996
Second week-day	72	377	113.73	.3017
Sunday	48	30	6.79	.2263
130TH STREET—P. S. Ry.				
First week-day	133	686	216.50	.3156
Second week-day	130	688	223.25	.3245
Sunday	157	651	205.45	.3156
TOTALS—All ferries, both ways.				
First week-day	2622	19158	5,274.90	.2753
Second week-day	2627	19131	5,276.45	.2758
Sunday	2040	5963	1,814.70	.3043

Total vehicular traffic over Hudson River Ferries for one year, based on average week-day record, multiplied by 300 for week-days and Sunday record, multiplied by 65 for Sundays and Holidays:

Ferry	Boats	Vehicles	Fares
Liberty Street, C. R. R.	91610	462840	$142,059.70
Cortlandt Street, P. R. R.	83005	650100	169,280.40
Cortlandt Street, W. S. R. R.	48480	277940	82,955.25
Barclay Street, D. L. & W. R. R.	82505	648930	152,808.55
Chambers Street, E. R. R.	73895	518190	140,988.85
Desbrosses Street, P. R. R.	89990	802355	240,710.30
Christopher Street, D., L. & W. W. R. R.	74685	444300	103,041.50
23rd Street, C. R. R.	38555	279050	90,242.65
23rd Street, D., L. & W. R. R.	69175	335475	87,666.90
23rd Street, E. R. R.	40490	377735	99,407.05
14th-23rd Streets, Hoboken	79200	437695	107,330.20
42nd Street, Weehawken, W. S. R. R.	72485	527020	168,654.55
42nd Street, W. N. Y., W. S. R. R.	26070	120900	36,195.35
130th Street, P. S. Ry.	49655	248415	79,316.75
Totals	919800	6130945	$1,700,658.00

Special information recorded during count:

Percentage fast moving to total vehicles, Week-days	14.8
Sundays	51.0
Average fare per vehicle, Week-days	27.56c
Sundays	30.43c
Average fare per vehicle	27.74c
Percentage Sunday to week-day business	34.4
Maximum number of vehicles per hour on ferries	797.
Income of ferries per Week-day	$5,275.68
Sunday	1,814.70

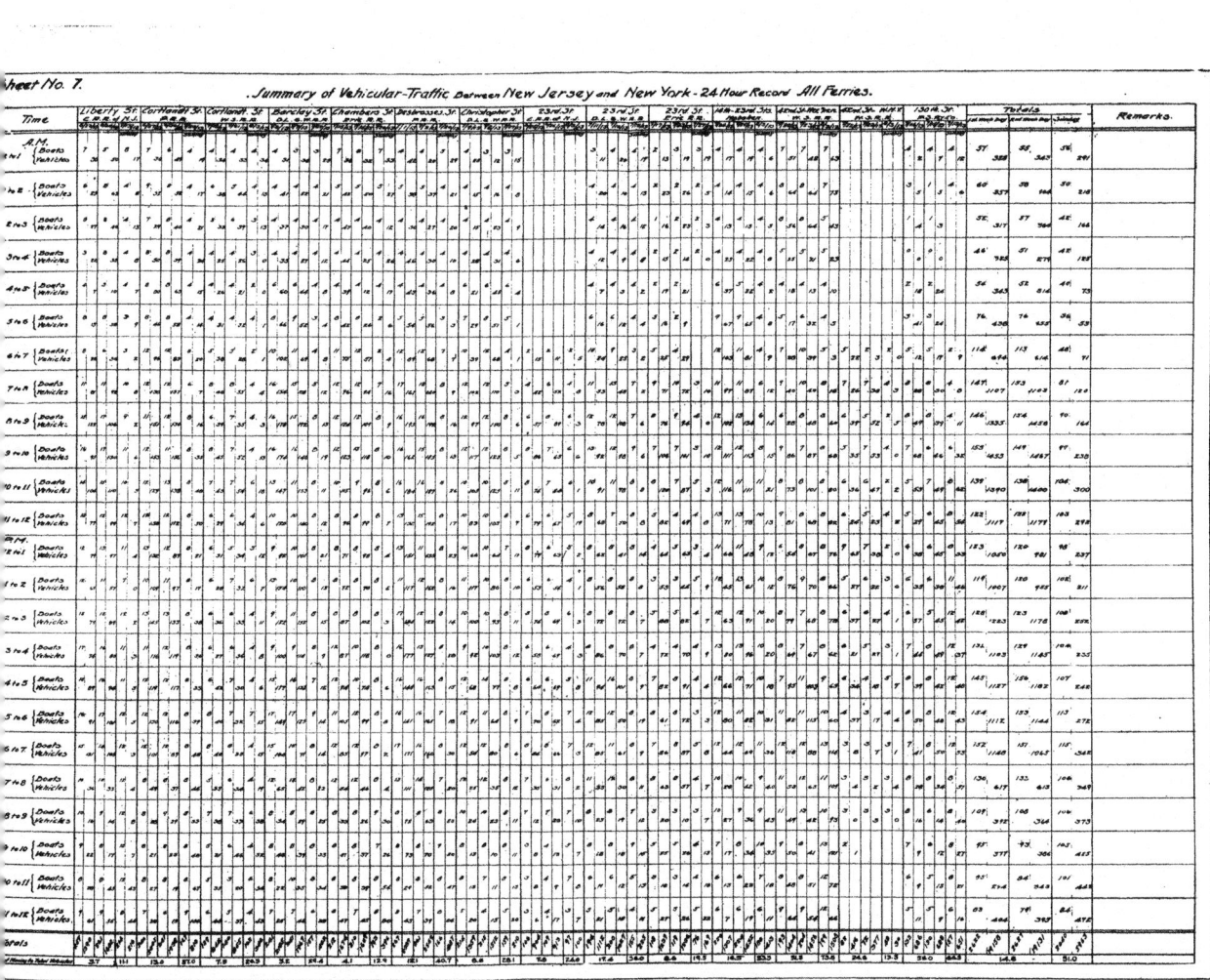

EXHIBIT 3.

TEN HOUR RECORD OF VEHICULAR TRAFFIC CROSSING THE HUDSON RIVER ON CORTLANDT STREET, BARCLAY STREET, CHAMBERS STREET, DESBROSSES STREET AND CHRISTOPHER STREET FERRIES.

TAKEN ON DECEMBER 18th AND 19th, 1916.

	Boats	Vehicles
CORTLANDT STREET—P. R. R.		
December 18, 1916	122	1476
" 19, "	129	1580
BARCLAY STREET—D., L. & W. R. R.		
December 18, 1916	130	1176
" 19, "	130	1299
CHAMBERS STREET—E. R. R.		
December 18, 1916	127	716
" 19, "	122	748
DESBROSSES STREET—P. R. R.		
December 18, 1916	98	2564
" 19, "	87	2308
CHRISTOPHER STREET—D., L. & W. R. R.		
December 18, 1916	110	805
" 19, "	110	1081
TOTALS.		
December 18, 1916	587	6737
" 19, "	578	7016

10-HOUR RECORD VEHICULAR TRAFFIC BETWEEN NEW JERSEY AND NEW YORK

TIME		Cortlandt St. P. R. R.		Barclay St. D.,L.&W.R.R.		Chambers St. Erie R. R.		Desbrosses St. P. R. R.		Christopher St. D.,L.&W.R.R.		Totals	
		12-18-16	12-19-16	12-18-16	12-19-16	12-18-16	12-19-16	12-18-16	12-19-16	12-18-16	12-19-16	12-18-16	12-19-16
8 to 9	Boats	13	13	15	15	13	13	10	11	12	12	63	64
	Vehicles	144	144	138	130	83	84	281	198	95	100	741	656
9 to 10	Boats	12	13	16	16	16	16	10	10	12	12	66	67
	Vehicles	150	169	141	142	82	87	202	317	73	132	648	847
10 to 11	Boats	12	14	12	12	14	14	9	7	10	10	57	57
	Vehicles	141	188	108	137	88	78	234	236	82	121	653	760
11 to 12	Boats	13	12	10	10	9	8	10	7	10	10	52	47
	Vehicles	181	162	122	130	79	105	234	289	84	118	700	804
1 to 2	Boats	11	13	9	9	7	7	9	7	10	10	46	46
	Vehicles	140	145	97	111	52	55	215	129	78	93	582	533
2 to 3	Boats	12	12	10	10	8	8	10	9	10	10	50	49
	Vehicles	163	157	112	132	76	74	258	195	87	120	696	678
3 to 4	Boats	12	12	10	10	12	12	10	9	10	10	54	53
	Vehicles	165	160	103	129	74	65	226	228	64	123	632	715
4 to 5	Boats	12	13	16	16	16	16	10	8	12	12	66	65
	Vehicles	137	178	129	138	75	67	231	228	91	89	663	700
5 to 6	Boats	12	14	16	16	16	16	9	10	12	12	65	68
	Vehicles	116	145	125	142	46	66	287	256	79	115	653	724
6 to 7	Boats	13	13	16	16	16	12	11	9	12	12	68	62
	Vehicles	139	132	101	108	61	67	396	222	72	70	769	599
Totals		122 1476	129 1580	130 1176	130 1299	127 716	122 748	98 2564	87 2308	110 805	110 1081	587 6737	578 7016

EXHIBIT 4.

MAP SHOWING PROPOSED TUNNEL

WITH RELATIVE LOCATION OF THE FIVE FERRIES

AND THE

NINE ARBITRARY TRAFFIC ZONES ON

EACH SIDE OF HUDSON RIVER.

Oversized Foldout

EXHIBIT 5.

RECORD OF TRAFFIC BETWEEN ZONES

VIA FERRIES AND BY PROPOSED TUNNEL

SHOWING COMPARATIVE DISTANCE AND TIME BY

FERRIES AND BY PROPOSED TUNNEL.

OPERATING DATA FOR MOTOR VEHICLES.

Between Zones		From New Jersey	Or To New York City	Via Ferry (Name)	Distance Feet	Total Distance	Time Minutes	Time on Land	Time Crossing River	Total Time	Distance Feet	Distance Ft. Tunnel	Total Distance	Time to Approach	Time thru Tunnel	Total Time	Total No. of Units	Minutes Saved by Using Tunnel	Increased Distance Travelled	Additional Cost per Unit
1	2	12 & Provost St.	John & Nassau Sts.	Barclay St.	N.J. 7500 / N.Y. 2500	10000	10½ / 7½	18	14	32	1000 / 7500	9500	18000	1 / 13	11	25	175	7	8000	.056
				Chambers St.	N.J. 5500 / N.Y. 3500	9000	7½ / 9½	17	12	29							609	4	9000	.063
1	4		W. B'dway & Grand	Chambers St.	N.J. 5500 / N.Y. 4500	0000	7½ / 9½	17	12	29	1000 / 2000	9500	12500	1 / 3½	11	15½	271	13½	2500	.0178
				Christopher St.	N.J. 7500 / N.Y. 8000	3500	10½ / 13½	24	12	36							41	20½	1000	.007
1	6		W. 11th & Hudson	Chambers St.	N.J. 5500 / N.Y. 8500	14000	7½ / 15½	23	12	35	1000 / 4500	9500	15000	1 / 7	11	19	25	16	1000	.007
				Christopher St.	N.J. 7500 / N.Y. 2500	10000	10½ / 4½	15	12	27							175	8	5000	.035
1	14		Jefferson & Cherry	Barclay St.	N.J. 7500 / N.Y. 8500	16000	10½ / 24½	35	14	49	1000 / 7500	9500	18000	1 / 16½	11	28½	14	20½	2000	.014
				Chambers St.	N.J. 5500 / N.Y. 8500	14000	7½ / 22½	30	12	42							48	13½	4000	.028
				Desbrosses St.	N.J. 8500 / N.Y. 9000	17500	10½ / 19½	30	17	47							7	16½	500	.0035
1	18		6th Ave. & 14th St.	Chambers St.	N.J. 5500 / N.Y. 11000	16500	7½ / 19½	27	2	39	1000 / 7000	9500	17500	1 / 14	11	25	41	14	1000	.007
				Christopher	N.J. 7500 / N.Y. 5000	12500	10½ / 8½	19	12	31							5	6	5000	.035
				Barclay St.	N.J. 7500 / N.Y. 12000	19500	10½ / 21½	32	14	46							4	21	2000	.014
3	2	Newark Ave. & Henderson St.	John & Nassau St.	Cortlandt St.	N.J. 3000 / N.Y. 2500	5500	4 / 5½	9½	13	22½	5000 / 7500	9500	22000	5½ / 13	11	29½	109	7	16500	.1155
				Desbrosses St.	N.J. 3000 / N.Y. 6500	9500	4 / 14½	18½	17	35½							193	6	12500	.0875
3	4		W. B'dway & Grand	Cortlandt St.	N.J. 3000 / N.Y. 6500	9500	4 / 13½	17½	13	30½	5000 / 2000	9500	16500	5½ / 3½	11	20	70	10½	7000	.049
				Desbrosses St.	N.J. 3000 / N.Y. 3000	6000	4 / 6½	10½	17	27½							314	7½	10500	.0735
3	6		W. 11th & Hudson	Desbrosses St.	N.J. 3000 / N.Y. 5500	8500	4 / 10½	14½	17	31½	5000 / 4500	9500	19000	5½ / 7	11	23½	129	8	10500	.0735
3	14		Jefferson & Cherry	Cortlandt St.	N.J. 3000 / N.Y. 9000	12000	4 / 26½	30½	13	43½	5000 / 7500	9500	22000	5½ / 16½	11	33	41	10½	10000	.07
				Desbrosses St.	N.J. 3000 / N.Y. 9000	12000	4 / 19½	23½	17	40½							19	7½	10000	.07
3	18		6th Ave. & 14th St.	Desbrosses St.	N.J. 3000 / N.Y. 8000	11000	4 / 14½	18½	17	35½	5000 / 7000	9500	21500	5½ / 14	11	30½	247	5	10500	.0735
5	2	Summit & Jewett Ave.	John & Nassau Sts.	Cortlandt Sts.	N.J. 12500 / N.Y. 2500	15000	18 / 5½	23½	13	36½	14500 / 7500	9500	31500	19 / 13	11	43	128	6½	16500	.1155
				Desbrosses St.	N.J. 12500 / N.Y. 6500	19000	18 / 14½	32½	17	49½							30	6½	21500	.1505
5	4		W. B'dway & Grand	Cortlandt St.	N.J. 12500 / N.Y. 6500	19000	18 / 13½	31½	13	44½	14500 / 2000	9500	26000	19 / 3½	11	33½	17	11	7000	.049
				Desbrosses St.	N.J. 12500 / N.Y. 3000	15500	18 / 6½	24½	17	41½							66	8	10500	.0735
7	2	Com'paw Ave. & Grand	John & Nassau St.	Cortlandt St.	N.J. 10500 / N.Y. 2500	13000	15 / 5½	20½	13	33½	12500 / 7500	9500	29500	16 / 13	11	40	134	6½	16500	.1155
				Desbrosses St.	N.J. 10500 / N.Y. 6500	17000	15 / 14½	29½	17	46½							37	6½	22500	.1575
9	2	Center Hackensack River and Plk. Rd. or Turnpike	John & Nassau St.	Cortlandt St. P.R.	N.J. 20000 / N.Y. 2500	22500	28 / 5½	33½	13	46½	22000 / 7500	9500	39000	29 / 13	11	53	493	6½	16500	.1155
				" " T.	N.J. 17500 / N.Y. 2500	20000	22 / 5½	27½	13	40½	12500 / 7500	9500	29500	14½ / 13	11	38½		2	9500	.0665
				Chambers St. P.R.	N.J. 24000 / N.Y. 3500	27500	32½ / 9½	42	12	54	22000 / 7500	9500	39000	29 / 13	11	53	51	1	11500	.0805
				" " T.	N.J. 17000 / N.Y. 3500	20500	21 / 9½	30½	12	42½	12500 / 7500	9500	29500	14½ / 13	11	38½		4	9000	.063
				Desbrosses St. P.R.	N.J. 20000 / N.Y. 6500	26500	28 / 14½	42½	17	59½	22000 / 7500	9500	39000	29 / 13	11	53	130	6½	2500	.0175
				" " T.	N.J. 17500 / N.Y. 6500	24000	22 / 14½	36½	17	53½	12500 / 7500	9500	29500	14½ / 13	11	38½		15	5500	.0385
9	4		W. B'dway & Grand	Cortlandt St. P.R.	N.J. 20000 / N.Y. 6500	26500	28 / 13½	41½	13	54½	22000 / 2000	9500	33500	29 / 3½	11	43½	56	11½	7000	.049
				" " T.	N.J. 17500 / N.Y. 6500	24000	22 / 13½	35½	13	48½	12500 / 2000	9500	24000	14½ / 3½	11	29		19½		.000
				Chambers St. P.R.	N.J. 24000 / N.Y. 4500	28500	32½ / 9½	42	12	54	22000 / 2000	9500	33500	29 / 3½	11	43½	32	10½	5000	.035
				" " T.	N.J. 17000 / N.Y. 4500	21500	21 / 9½	30½	12	42½	12500 / 2000	9500	24000	14½ / 3½	11	29		13½	2500	.0175
				Desbrosses St. P.R.	N.J. 20000 / N.Y. 3000	23000	28 / 6½	34½	17	51½	22000 / 2000	9500	33500	29 / 3½	11	43½	155	8	10500	.0735
				" " T.	N.J. 17500 / N.Y. 3000	20500	22 / 6½	28½	17	45½	12500 / 2000	9500	24000	14½ / 3½	11	29		16½	3500	.0245
9	6		W. 11th St. & Hudson	Chambers St. P.R.	N.J. 24000 / N.Y. 8500	32500	32½ / 15½	48	12	60	22000 / 4500	9500	36000	29 / 7	11	47	6	13	3500	.0245
				" " T.	N.J. 17000 / N.Y. 8500	25500	21 / 15½	36½	12	48½	12500 / 4500	9500	26500	14½ / 7	11	32½		16	1000	.007
				Desbrosses St. P.R.	N.J. 20000 / N.Y. 5500	25500	28 / 10½	38½	17	55½	22000 / 4500	9500	36000	29 / 7	11	47	47	8½	10500	.0735
				" " T.	N.J. 17500 / N.Y. 5500	23000	22 / 10½	32½	17	49½	12500 / 4500	9500	26500	14½ / 7	11	32½		17	3500	.0245
				Christopher St. P.R.	N.J. 28000 / N.Y. 2500	30500	38½ / 4½	43	12	55	22000 / 4500	9500	36000	29 / 7	11	47	28	8	5500	.0385
				" " T.	N.J. 18500 / N.Y. 2500	21000	23 / 4½	27½	12	39½	12500 / 4500	9500	26500	14½ / 7	11	32½		7	5500	.0385
9	18		6th Ave. & 14th St.	Chambers St. P.R.	N.J. 24000 / N.Y. 11000	35000	32½ / 19½	52	12	64	22000 / 7000	9500	38500	29 / 14	11	54	6	10	3500	.0245
				" " T.	N.J. 17000 / N.Y. 11000	28000	21 / 19½	40½	12	52½	12500 / 7000	9500	29000	14½ / 14	11	39½		13	1000	.007
				Desbrosses St. P.R.	N.J. 20000 / N.Y. 8000	28000	28 / 14½	42½	17	59½	22000 / 7000	9500	38500	29 / 14	11	54	86	3½	10500	.0735
				" " T.	N.J. 17500 / N.Y. 8000	25500	22 / 14½	36½	17	53½	12500 / 7000	9500	29000	14½ / 14	11	39½		14	3500	.0245
				Christopher St. P.R.	N.J. 28000 / N.Y. 5000	33000	38½ / 8½	47	12	59	22000 / 7000	9500	38500	29 / 14	11	54	6	5	5500	.0385
				" " T.	N.J. 18500 / N.Y. 5000	23500	23 / 8½	31½	12	43½	12500 / 7000	9500	29000	14½ / 14	11	39½		4	5500	.0385
13	2	Palisade & Ravine Ave.	John & Nassau Sts.	Barclay St.	N.J. 6500 / N.Y. 2500	9000	12 / 7½	19½	14	33½	4500 / 7500	9500	22500	10½ / 13	11	34½	1136	1	13500	.0945
				Christopher St.	N.J. 6500 / N.Y. 10000	16500	12 / 20½	32½	12	44½							189	10	6000	.042
13	4		W. B'dway & Grand	Barclay St.	N.J. 6500 / N.Y. 5500	12000	12 / 11½	23½	14	37½	4500 / 2000	9500	16000	10½ / 3½	11	25	137	12½	4000	.028
				Christopher St.	N.J. 6500 / N.Y. 6000	12500	12 / 13½	25½	12	37½							346	12½	4500	.0315
13	6		W. 11th St. & Hudson St.	" "	N.J. 6500 / N.Y. 2500	9000	12 / 4½	16½	12	28½	4500 / 4500	9500	18500	10½ / 7	11	28½	414		9500	.0665
13	8		University Pl. W. 7th	" "	N.J. 6500 / N.Y. 5000	11500	12 / 9	21	12	33	4500 / 3500	9500	19500	10½ / 16	11	37½	65	4½	8000	.056
13	14		Jefferson & Cherry	Barclay St.	N.J. 6500 / N.Y. 8500	13000	12 / 24½	36½	14	50½	4500 / 7500	9500	21500	10½ / 16½	11	37½	44	13	6500	.0455
				Christopher St.	N.J. 6500 / N.Y. 11500	18000	12 / 25½	37½	12	49½							22	12	3500	.0245
13	18		6th Ave. & 14th St.	Barclay St.	N.J. 6500 / N.Y. 12000	18500	12 / 21½	33½	14	47½	4500 / 7000	9500	21000	10½ / 14	11	35½	17	12	2500	.0175
				Christopher St.	N.J. 6500 / N.Y. 5000	11500	12 / 8½	20½	12	32½							94	3	9500	.0665
																	7089			

Total units interviewed: 8140
Zone combinations: 405
All zones showing less than 50 units and zones which showed little or no movement of units eliminated reducing to 7089 units or 87% of total and 48 zones.
Zone 9 can be reached by (2) two ways.
About ⅓ of units interviewed came from or went west of Hackensack River (or zone 9).

	10 Ton	7 Ton	5 Ton	3 Ton	2 Ton	1 Ton
Depreciation	780.00	743.00	695.00	421.00	390.00	225.00
Tires	1630.00	1231.00	930.00	620.00	480.00	300.00
Yearly overhaul & current repair	550.00	500.00	450.00	400.00	350.00	300.00
Gas at 17¢ per gal.	637.50	637.50	637.50	531.25	459.42	389.53
Oil " 30¢ " qt.	120.00	100.00	90.00	60.00	50.00	40.00
Yearly cost	3737.50	3211.50	2802.50	2032.25	1729.42	1254.53
Daily " (300)	12.46	10.71	9.34	6.74	5.76	4.18
Daily miles av.	.38	46	.50	.60	.70	.80
Cost per mile	.33	23	.19	.11	.08	.05

10 Ton		0.33
7	"	0.23
5	"	0.19
3	"	0.11
2	"	0.08
1	"	0.05
28	"	0.99

0.99 ÷ 28 = 0.353+ say $.007 per 1000 ft. per ton. Applying this to vehicular traffic investigation we have as average increased cost in using tunnel by the 7089 units if vehicles came from zone 9 via Plank Road of $0.074 per ton via Turnpike $0.068 per ton via ½ and ½ $0.071.

Average saving } 7.8 minutes by P.R. 8.8 minutes by T. ½ & ½ 8.4

Average increase } P.R. 7844 } 0.0548; T. 6969 0.0488; ½ and ½ 7406 0.0518. Avg. additional cost per zone per unit.

During March 1918 drivers of horse and motor trucks crossing Cortlandt Street, Barclay Street, Chambers Street, Desbrosses Street and Christopher Street ferries in both directions were interviewed and information as to starting and destination points of each truck and rated tonnage of each obtained.... One ton was adopted as a unit and the movement of traffic recorded in units.... Nine zones were laid out on each side of the river and traffic between zones with ferry used plotted.... Experimental runs with a two ton truck were made from the center of each zone to each ferry and to the proposed tunnel entrance and the time consumed and distance carefully recorded.

In calculating time by ferry the actual time of reaching the ferry from zone center plus one half of the headway of boats to cover average waits, the actual time of crossing the river and the actual time required to reach the center of zone on opposite side were included.......... In calculating time by tunnel the actual time of reaching the tunnel plus the tunnel distance at 10 miles per hour and the actual time of reaching the zone center on the other side were included.......

The cost of operating a ton mile was based on gasoline at 17¢ and other costs as shown averaged for trucks from one to ten tons........ The final figures show the saving of time by tunnel for an average vehicle from zone center to zone center and the additional cost of operating an average ton by way of the tunnel.

G.M.B. Nov. 29 1918 — C.E.M. Dec. 14 18

EXHIBIT 6.

REPORT ON

TUNNELS UNDER THE RIVER THAMES,

LONDON, ENGLAND.

Tunnels Under the River Thames

One of London's most important problems is that which concerns the provision of facilities for communication between the districts situated on either side of the River Thames. Such communication has been found necessary from very early times, and with the extension of the population along the banks of the river, the need has correspondingly increased. The census of 1911 gives the population of Greater London as 7,251,358, of which number 2,542,666 lived south of the River Thames.

London Bridge marks the head of navigation by ocean-going vessels, and above that point facilities for communication have been fairly well supplied by the construction of bridges. Below London Bridge, however, until the opening of the Blackwall and Rotherhithe Tunnels, the facilities provided did not in the least correspond with the requirements. The districts east of the river had developed rapidly; businesses of vast extent and docks of great importance had located along both banks of the river, between which there was constant traffic communication. Ferries were established here and there, but were considered objectionable because of the narrowness of the Thames, and the consequent interference with navigation. Many schemes for bridges were suggested, but considered impracticable, and with the single exception of the Tower Bridge, a bascule draw, opened in 1894 near the head of navigation, none were constructed.

As bridges were impracticable, and ferries undesirable, much attention was given to the subject of tunnels, and so long ago as 1798, a start was made on a tunnel designed to connect Tilbury with Gravesend. This tunnel was, however, never completed because of difficulties encountered in financing it.

In 1805 a tunnel between Limehouse and Rotherhithe was started, but after being nearly completed, the roof collapsed, and the work was abandoned.

In 1825 work on the Thames Pedestrian Tunnel, connecting Wapping and Rotherhithe, was commenced, and in 1843 completed. This tunnel, the first ever built by the shield method, is 1,200 feet long, and consists of two arched passageways. It was used as a pedestrian tunnel until 1866, when it was sold to the East London Railway Company, for use as a railway tunnel.

In 1870 the Tower Subway was opened to pedestrians, but, for some reason, closed in 1897.

In 1876 another pedestrian subway was started between North and South Woolwich, but never completed.

THE BLACKWALL TUNNEL.

About the year 1875 it became generally recognized that the construction of more river crossings below London Bridge could not be further delayed, and the matter was taken up by the Metropolitan Board of Works, who brought forward several schemes for bridges and tunnels, but it was not until 1887 that the Blackwall Tunnel Act was obtained. At this time there was no free crossing provided for vehicles between London Bridge and the Woolwich Free Ferry, a distance of 9½ miles.

Cost. The tunnel was begun in 1892 and completed in 1897. It was designed by Mr. Alexander R. Binnie, Chief Engineer of the London County Council and built by Messrs. S. Pearson & Son.

The contract price was	£870,000
Cost of property	355,000
Cost of sites for rehousing	83,000
Miscellaneous	98,000
Total cost	£1,406,000

Location. The Blackwall Tunnel is located about six and one-quarter miles below London Bridge, and connects the Boroughs of Poplar and Greenwich, and the sections of these Boroughs known respectively as Blackwall and East Greenwich. The line of the tunnel is irregular, the changes in direction being made by angles at the shafts, instead of by curving. The changes in the direction of the tunnel, and the apparently unnecessary length of the land portions were made to avoid, as far as possible, docks and other surface improvements, and at the same time to provide entrances adjacent to main highways.

General Description. The Blackwall Tunnel consists of a shield driven, iron lined tube, having an outside diameter of 27 feet, with an inside diameter of 24 feet and 3 inches. It is lined with concrete faced with glazed white tile, and has a roadway sixteen feet between curbs, with two footpaths each 3 feet 1½ inches wide. The maximum gradient of the roadway is 1 foot in 36 feet. The headroom in the tunnel varies from 15 feet 6 inches to 17 feet 7½ inches, and the gauge for vehicles at the entrances is fixed at 15 feet 6 inches. The lengths of the several sections are as follows:

Open cut northerly entrance to north portal	875	ft.
North portal to shaft No. 1	1257	"
Shaft No. 1 to shaft No. 2	444	"
Shaft No. 2 to shaft No. 3 (river portion)	1220	"
Shaft No. 3 to shaft No. 4	598	"
Shaft No. 4 to south portal	946	"
Open cut from south portal to south entrance	860	"
Total length	6200	"

At each vehicle entrance there is a stone lodge, providing offices and living quarters for some of the tunnel attendants. Four shafts break the

HIGHWAY, ADJACENT TO POPLAR ENTRANCE TO BLACKWALL TUNNEL

line of the tunnel, each 48 feet in internal diameter, the locations of which were determined by the changes in the direction of the tunnel. The shafts on the river banks are used as entrances for pedestrians, and in each there is a circular iron stairway of 100 easy steps, with safety treads, leading to the surface. In addition to these entrances, staircases are constructed at the portals; thus providing three entrances for pedestrians on each side of the river. These entrances are used extensively by employees of adjacent docks and manufactories.

THE SAME HIGHWAY SHOWING POPLAR ENTRANCE LODGE

POPLAR ENTRANCE TO BLACKWALL TUNNEL

GREENWICH ENTRANCE TO BLACKWALL TUNNEL

A NEAR VIEW OF GREENWICH ENTRANCE

Paving. The roadway on the level stretches is paved with sheet asphalt, which in slippery weather is kept well sanded. The gradients are paved with stone block, on which, during freezing weather, a heavy gravel is freely used. An experimental wood block pavement has recently been laid on one of the gradients, and the result is so satisfactory that the Tunnel Superintendent recommends wood block throughout, in preference to the very noisy stone block.

Lighting. When the tunnel was constructed, a lighting plant was installed, and the tunnel was then lighted by three rows of incandescent lamps, spaced 15 feet apart in each row. This lighting was found to be more than was necessary, and the lighting plant proved very costly. The plant was subsequently shut down, and a single row of 50 candle power incandescent lamps are now used. As a measure of safety, two lighting circuits are installed with separate sources of supply, alternate lights being on the same circuit. While the lighting of the tunnel is by no means brilliant, the white tiled walls serve as reflectors, and the result is quite satisfactory.

BLACKWALL TUNNEL. SHOWING SINGLE ROW OF LIGHTS AND REFLECTION FROM TILED WALLS.

Ventilation. The only ventilation is provided by the open ends and the four circular shafts. These shafts are covered with glass domed roofs. The two shafts located directly on the banks of the river have grilled openings directly beneath the dome about 10 feet high, and the full circumference of the shaft. The other two shafts are entirely closed, except for openings about three feet in diameter in the centre of the domes. The ventilation supplied by these several openings, while inadequate today, is said to have been sufficient before the extensive use of the tunnel by motors.

Before the war, means of better ventilation were under consideration, and something will, no doubt, soon be done to improve conditions. Artificial ventilation was considered during the construction of the tunnel, and space for air ducts was provided beneath the roadway, although no definite plan for ventilation seems to have been made.

Conduits and Pipes Under Roadway. Under the roadway, ducts are provided to carry tramway cables from municipally-owned power house on the south, to a substation on the north, also post office telephone wires, cables for tunnel light and power, mains for tunnel water, and tunnel drainage pipes. Entrance to these is provided by manholes at the shafts.

Drainage. The tunnel is drained by small grating covered catch-basins set in the gutters of the roadway about 100 feet apart. The basins connected with a 6-inch drain pipe under the roadway on the gradients, and with a 9-inch pipe under the level sections. These pipes drain into a sump tank holding 1,000 gallons, located below the bottom level of the tunnel in shaft #2. The total seepage of the tunnel is about 300 gallons daily. The seepage beneath the roadway is collected in a gutter in the bottom of the tube, which discharges into the sump tank. The seepage from the sides of the tunnel is collected in a drain back of the glazed brick lining just above the sidewalk, and reaches the roadway drains across the sidewalk by means of small gulleys 200 feet apart. These gulleys are cleaned every two weeks, while the catch-basins and drain pipes are cleaned every two months.

Pumping Plant. The pumping plant, consisting of three 15 H. P. deep well electric pumps is located in shaft #2, near the top, in order to be in a position to pump out the whole tunnel, in case it should become flooded. The pumps discharge directly into the Thames. One pump used about six hours per day serves ordinarily, although about six times per year, during heavy rains, all three are used.

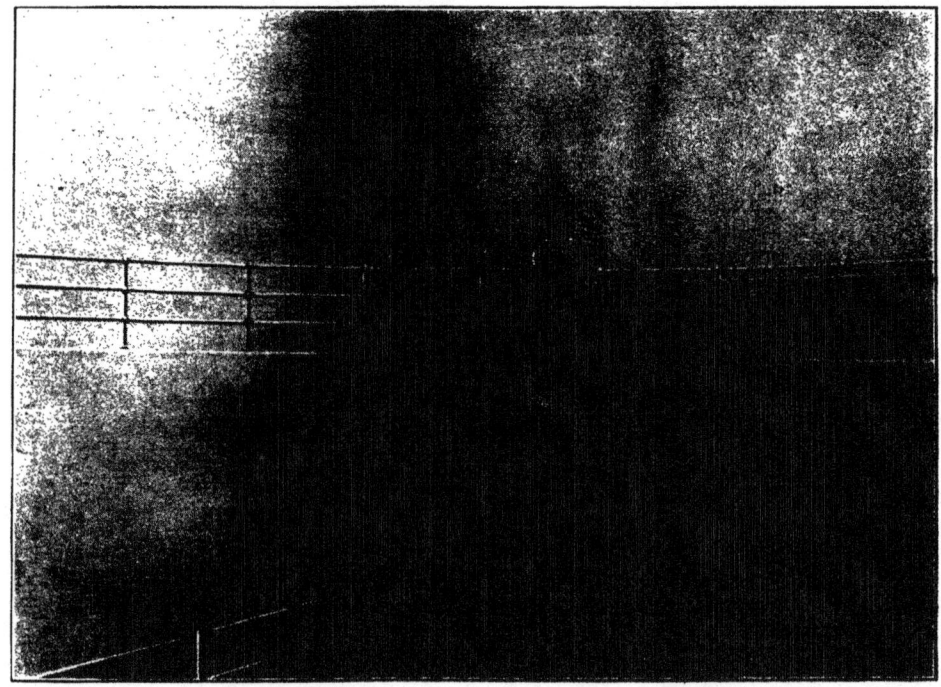

PUMPING PLANT LOCATED NEAR HEAD OF SHAFT.

Tunnel Cleaning. The tunnel is cleaned three times per week by flushing roadways, sidewalks and walls, and glazed brick is scrubbed with a broom to the height that a man can reach. Work is always done after eleven o'clock in the evening. Water for this purpose is supplied from wall hydrants located from one hundred to two hundred feet apart. The superintendent reports that after cleaning, it requires twenty-four hours to become thoroughly dry.

Policing. The tunnel is regular policed by four men, one on fixed post at each vehicle entrance, and two patrolmen inside. The men alternating in and out generally on four hour shifts. Ventilation has of recent years become so difficult, due to increase in the number of motors, that on days when the air is particularly bad, the police alternate on one hour shifts.

Telephones. The tunnel is provided with telephones at each entrance lodge and at the pump houses.

Traffic Regulations. The Blackwall Tunnel is operated by the London County Council, and traffic in it is subject to the following rules:

1. Any person who shall ride on horseback, or drive or conduct any cart, carriage or other vehicle into or through the tunnel shall keep to the left side of the road, and shall, unless prevented by traffic or other unavoidable cause, proceed without stopping. Provided that this by-law shall not be deemed to prohibit the stoppage of a vehicle for such time as may be necessary for the purpose of taking up or setting down any passengers who may require to be taken up or set down.

2. Any person passing on foot through the tunnel shall, unless otherwise directed by the police on duty, keep to the footway on the right side of the tunnel.

3. No person shall go down any of the steps, or any part of any spiral staircase, provided for the purpose of exit from the tunnel.

4. No person shall go up any of the steps, or any part of any spiral staircase, provided for the purpose of entry to the tunnel.

5. No person who shall ride on horseback, or drive or conduct any cart, carriage or other vehicle into or through the tunnel, shall turn such horse, cart, carriage or other vehicle, or pass or attempt to pass any horse, cart, carriage or other vehicle, in such a manner as to interfere in any way with foot passengers, or the space to be used by foot passengers, or with any horse, cart, carriage or other vehicle proceeding in the opposite direction.

6. No person shall drive or conduct into the tunnel any cart, carriage or other vehicle which shall not (with its load if any) pass through without touching the gauge erected at the entrance of the tunnel.

7. No person shall drive or conduct into or through the tunnel any cart, carriage, or other vehicle, which is not provided with sufficient and reliable brakes or skids, and with such animal or mechanical power as when ascending any gradient will prevent obstruction of or interference with any other cart, carriage or other vehicle which may be in the tunnel.

8. No person shall drive or conduct into or through the tunnel any cart, carriage or other vehicle laden with timber, metal, or any other article which exceeds in length 25 feet, or which protrudes more than 8 feet behind the vehicle.

9. No person shall drive or conduct into or through the tunnel any vehicle the weight of which when loaded shall exceed 5 tons on any wheel.

10. No person shall drive or conduct any vehicle propelled by mechanical power into or through the tunnel at a greater speed than—
   (I) In the case of vehicles of or under two tons in weight unladen —eight miles per hour.
   (II) In the case of vehicles over two tons in weight unladen—six miles per hour.
   (III) In the case of vehicles drawing a trailer—four miles an hour.

Provided that this by-law shall not authorize a greater speed in respect of any heavy motor car within the meaning of the Heavy Motor Car Order, 1904, than is permitted by such order.

The weight of any vehicle unladen for the purpose of this by-law means the weight of such vehicle exclusive of the weight of any water, fuel or accumulators used for the purpose of propulsion.

11. No person shall drive or conduct into or through the tunnel any cattle or any animal forming part of a menagerie, or any wild animal, unless such animal shall be under proper control.

12. No person shall take into the tunnel any loaded firearm or any explosive within the meaning of the Explosives Act, 1875, or any petroleum to which the Petroleum Act, 1871, applies, or any corrosive acid or other substance, whether similar to those above mentioned or not, which may cause injury or fire or explosion in the tunnel or prejudicially effect the use of the tunnel or cause or be likely to cause any danger to any person in or using the tunnel. Provided that this by-law shall not apply to safety cartridges, safety fuses for blasting, railway fog signals or percussion caps. Provided also that this by-law shall not prohibit the conveyance through the tunnel of petroleum which is being used on a motor vehicle for the purpose only of the propulsion of such vehicle, or which is being carried on a motor vehicle for such use.

13. No person shall climb upon or do damage to the structure of the tunnel, or any of the entrance gates or gateways, or remove or damage any of the railings, fences, seats, staircases, stairs, barriers, gates, lamps, lamp posts, pipes, telephone boxes, wires, notice boards, machinery or other matters or things in or appurtenant to the tunnel, or post any bill, placard or notice, or write, stamp, cut, print, draw or make marks in any manner on any part thereof.

14. No person shall commit any nuisance contrary to public decency or propriety in the tunnel.

15. No person shall drive or conduct into or through the tunnel any cart or other vehicle carrying any faecal or offensive or noxious matter or liquid, or any vehicle (except a fire-engine) emitting smoke or visible vapour so as in any manner to be a nuisance or to endanger, or to be likely to endanger, the safety or interfere with the convenience of any person using the tunnel.

16. Any person who shall offend against any of the foregoing by-laws shall be liable for each breach of such by-laws, to a penalty not exceeding forty shillings, and in case of a continuing offence to a further penalty not exceeding twenty shillings for each day after notice of the offence from the Council.

N. B.—The foregoing by-laws are intended to be in addition to and not in derogation of the provisions of any enactment relating to highways or streets.

In addition to these special regulations, the rules governing traffic on the streets of London also apply. Of these general traffic rules, the only one of particular interest prohibits the use of any car, the width of which between extreme projecting points measures more than seven feet six inches.

Amount of Traffic. Statistics published by the London County Council give the number of passengers and vehicles using the Blackwall Tunnel in recent years, as follows:

Year	Passengers	Vehicles
1898	4,155,890	335,425
1902	4,599,395	820,449
1905	3,741,542	924,399
1906	4,086,460	983,075
1907	3,736,818	984,978
1908	3,278,262	827,160
1909	3,599,769	933,116
1910	3,503,166	836,736
1911	3,756,658	808,553
1912	3,114,600	736,500
1913	3,742,241	772,940

These figures show some reduction in traffic after the opening of the Rotherhithe Tunnel in 1908. Figures for 1914 and 1915 have not been compiled.

The London traffic branch of the Board of Trade publish the following statistics of traffic in the Blackwall Tunnel for an average day in 1913 and in 1914 between the hours of 8 A. M. and 8 P. M., while the comparative figures for January 27 and 28, 1916, were furnished by the Clerk of the London County Council and cover from 6 A. M. to 7 P. M.

	1913	1914	Jan. 27, 1916	Jan. 28, 1916
TRADE VEHICLES:				
1 horse, fast	357.	320.	....	....
slow	322.	404.	747.	826.
2 horses or more				
fast	102	90.	....	....
slow	222.	165.	382.	399.
Motor, fast	65.	78.	....	....
slow	44.	54.	341.	397.
Total	1112.	1111.	1470.	1622.
PASSENGER VEHICLES:				
Omnibuses, horse	....	....	....	....
motor	458.	289.	267.	231.
Cabs, horse	....	2.	6.	2.
motor	6.	....	11.	2.
Carriages, horse	19.	21.	12.	11.
motor	49.	70.	100.	132.
Total	532.	382.	396.	378.
Total horse and motor vehicles	1644.	1493.	1866.	2000.
Barrows	31.	16.	13.	13.
Cycles, ordinary	380.	378.	197.	154.
motor	16.	13.	8.	3.
Total traffic both ways	2071.	1900.	2084.	2170.

NUMERICAL COMPARISON OF HORSE AND MOTOR VEHICLES

	1913 %	1914 %	Jan. 27, 1916 %	Jan. 28, 1916 %
Percentage of horse vehicles in trade vehicles	90.	88.	76.	75.
Percentage of horse vehicles in passenger vehicles	4.	6.	4.	4.
Percentage of horse vehicles in total horse and motor vehicles	62.	67.	61.	62.
Percentage of trade vehicles in total (excluding cycles and barrows)	68.	74.	78.	80.

TRAFFIC BY HOURS, JANUARY 27, 1916

HOUR	Number of Vehicles, excluding barrows and cycles			Total, including cycles, etc.	Number of Persons in or with vehicles and on foot		
	North to South	South to North	Total		North to South	South to North	Total
A. M.							
5 to 6	......	......	......	......	125	56	181
6 to 7	15	14	29	59	424	199	623
7 to 8	28	33	61	92	332	230	562
8 to 9	58	53	111	140	272	332	604
9 to 10	100	84	184	194	243	233	476
10 to 11	99	67	166	176	235	228	463
11 to 12	101	90	191	195	268	250	518
P. M.							
12 to 1	110	80	190	199	272	221	493
1 to 2	83	86	169	178	253	286	539
2 to 3	75	61	136	142	235	213	448
3 to 4	95	81	176	185	288	243	631
4 to 5	112	71	183	198	328	313	641
5 to 6	71	91	162	196	378	467	845
6 to 7	35	73	108	130	198	388	586
Total	982	884	1866	2084	3851	3659	7510

TRAFFIC BY HOURS, JANUARY 28, 1916

HOUR	Number of Vehicles, excluding barrows and cycles			Total, including cycles, etc.	Number of Persons in or with vehicles and on foot		
	North to South	South to North	Total		North to South	South to North	Total
A. M.							
5 to 6	......	......	......	......	117	62	179
6 to 7	13	14	27	46	369	206	575
7 to 8	31	33	64	88	359	244	603
8 to 9	70	59	129	138	262	299	561
9 to 10	80	65	145	153	190	210	400
10 to 11	113	78	191	196	251	199	450
11 to 12	106	76	182	186	241	186	427
P. M.							
12 to 1	126	78	204	210	287	195	482
1 to 2	75	77	152	161	200	242	442
2 to 3	80	66	146	149	200	217	417
3 to 4	105	84	189	197	258	244	502
4 to 5	74	99	173	194	336	384	720
5 to 6	100	119	219	248	439	485	924
6 to 7	65	114	179	204	296	495	791
Total	1038	962	2000	2170	3805	3668	7473

Operating Staff. The staff of the Blackwall Tunnel consists of
- 1 Superintendent,
- 1 Deputy Superintendent,
- 1 Store and General Clerk,

who also have charge of the Rotherhithe Tunnel, the Greenwich Pedestrian Tunnel, and the Deptford Creek Bridge. The following are exclusively employed in the Blackwall Tunnel:
- 1 Foreman Laborer,
- 8 Laborers,
- 5 Orderly Boys,
- 4 Electrical Fitters,
- 1 Drainage Pump Attendant,
- 1 Lamp Man.

Of the laborers employed, six men work from 11 P. M. until 9 A. M. six nights per week, in flushing walls and roadway, and in cleaning drains, etc. The remaining two men are employed during the day upon the roadway and in general work. The orderly boys are employed during the day in keeping the roadway clean. The electrical fitters are engaged in maintenance of electrical work, two being on duty at night.

Operating Cost. The average annual cost of operating the Blackwall Tunnel is as follows:

Salaries and Wages	£1800
Removal of road sweepings, sprinkling roadway when needed, supplying 300 yards of gravel and 20 yards of sand for gradients in winter	311
Water for cleaning	115
Electricity for lighting and pumping	800
Supplies including lamp renewals	250
	£3276

The expense of policing the tunnel is not included. In addition to the above, the London County Council charge about £2,000 annually to tunnel maintenance to represent engineering and general administration expenses.

Greenwich Pedestrian Subway. After the opening of the Blackwall Tunnel, a pedestrian tunnel to connect Greenwich and the Isle of Dogs, about one and one-half miles above the Blackwall Tunnel, was constructed and opened in 1902. This tunnel cost £180,000 including land purchases. It is 1217 feet long, 12 feet 9 inches in external diameter, with a footway of 9 feet and headroom varying from 7 feet 6 inches to 9 feet 4½ inches. Entrance is provided at the river banks by two shafts 32 feet 8 inches in diameter, in each of which is an electric elevator, having a capacity of 100 persons. This tunnel is used by 7,000,000 persons annually, of whom 5,000,000 use the elevators.

Due to the constant operation of the two large elevators the annual operating cost of this tunnel is about £3,000.

ROTHERHITHE TUNNEL.

The next step toward furnishing better means of communication between north and south London, was taken in 1900, when an act was passed authorizing the construction of a vehicular tunnel about two and one quarter miles below London Bridge, to connect the Boroughs of Stepney and Bermondsey, and the districts known respectively as Ratcliff and Rotherhithe.

Cost. This tunnel was begun in 1904 and completed in 1908. It was designed by Mr. Maurice Fitz Maurice, Chief Engineer of the London County Council, and built by Messrs. Price and Reeves.

The contract price was	£1,088,484
The cost of property, sites for rehousing and miscellaneous approximately	911,516
Approximate total cost	£2,000,000

Like the Blackwall Tunnel, this tunnel is irregular in line, crosses the river obliquely, and extends a considerable distance on land to escape important docks, and to reach main highways.

General Description. In design, the Rotherhithe Tunnel closely resembles the Blackwall Tunnel; the principal difference being an increase of three feet in diameter. The roadway is sixteen feet between curbs, the same as the Blackwall roadway, the additional available width being given to the footpaths, which are 4 feet 8½ inches wide. The maximum gradient is 1 foot in 37 feet. The headroom being greater than in the Blackwall Tunnel, the gauge at the entrance is fixed at 17 feet. This tunnel is also lined with white glazed brick.

The lengths of the several sections are as follows:

Open cut northerly portal to northerly entrance	1186 ft.
Brick cut and cover shaft No. 4 to northerly portal	600 "
Iron lined shaft No. 3 to shaft No. 4	1155 "
Iron lined shaft No. 2 to shaft No. 3 (river portions)	1535 "
Iron lined shaft No. 1 to shaft No. 2	890 "
Brick cut and cover southerly portal to shaft No. 1	530 "
Open cut south entrance to southerly portal	930 "
Total length	6826 "

At each vehicle entrance, a half section of the steel cutting edge used in the construction of the tunnel is erected, from which is suspended the gauge measuring the height of vehicles.

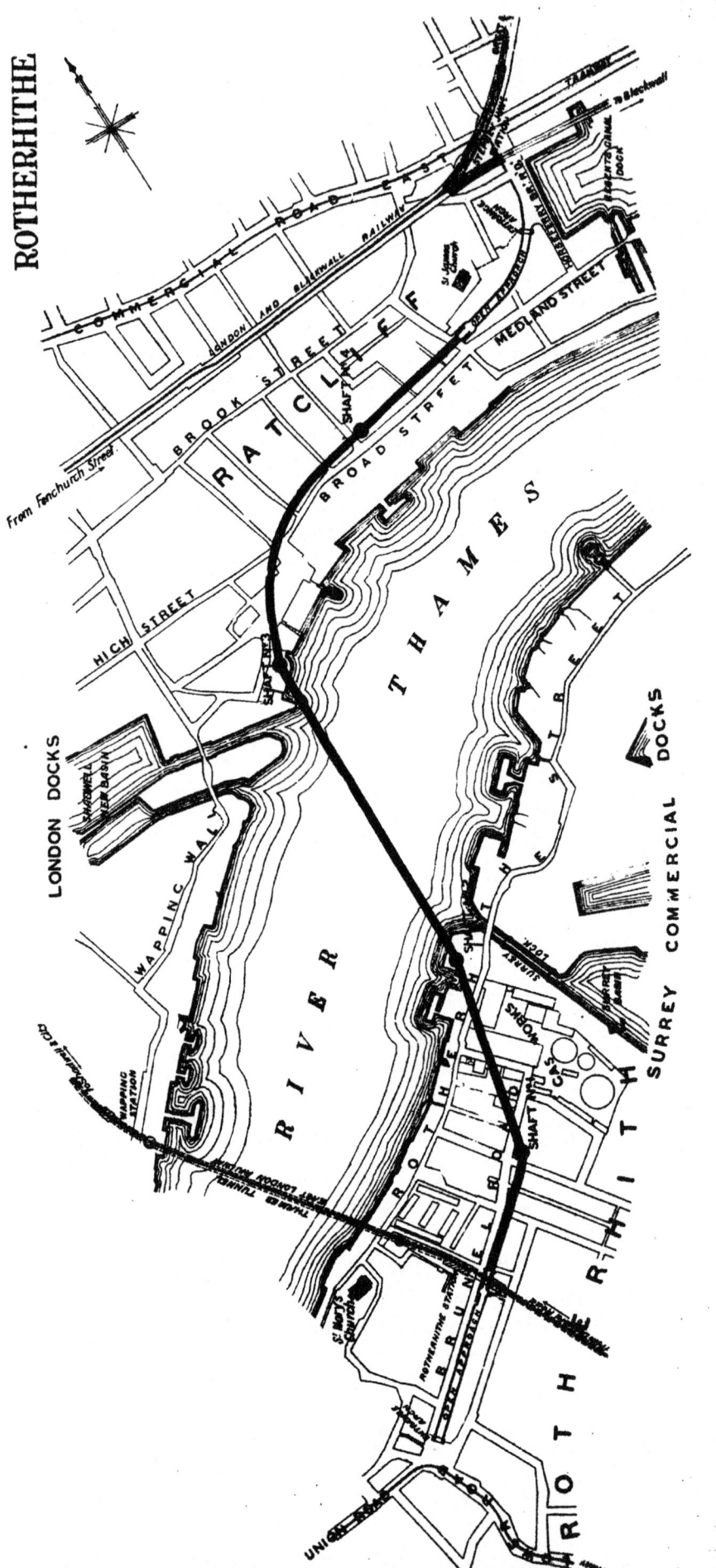

The four shafts breaking the line of tunnel are each 50 feet in internal diameter. Those on the river banks are used as entrances for pedestrians and in each there is a circular iron stairway leading to the surface. In addition to these entrances, staircases are provided at the portals, thus providing in all, six entrances for pedestrians.

COMMERCIAL ROAD, STEPNEY, AND ENTRANCE TO ROTHERHITHE TUNNEL

Paving. The roadway is paved with sheet asphalt on the level portions and stone block on the gradients, and is in every way similar to the Blackwall Tunnel.

Lighting. The tunnel is lighted by three rows of 25 C. P. incandescent lamps, staggered thirty feet apart in each row, two rows of which are always used. The illumination obtained is considerably better than in the Blackwall Tunnel.

Ventilation. The only ventilation is provided by the open ends, and the four circular shafts. The shafts on the river bank are covered with domed glass roofs with side openings similar to openings in the Blackwall Tunnel shafts, while the other two shafts have open tops—a considerable improvement over similarly located shafts in the Blackwall Tunnel.

Conduits and Pipes Under Roadway. The roadway is supported on a brick arch built up from the bottom of the tube, and a considerable space under this

PORTAL OF ROTHERHITHE TUNNEL, SHOWING STAIRWAY FOR PEDESTRIANS

arch is available for pipes. It is used, however, only for electric light and telephone conduits, and water mains for the tunnel itself.

Drainage. The drainage system of the Rotherhithe Tunnel is very similar to that of the Blackwall Tunnel previously described, except that drainage pipes are 12 inches in diameter, and the sump tank holds 3,000 gallons. The total seepage of this tunnel is only about 100 gallons daily.

LOWER ROAD, ROTHERHITHE AND ENTRANCE TO TUNNEL

ROTHERHITHE ENTRANCE TO TUNNEL

PORTION OF THE COMPLETED TUNNEL

BEGINNING OF OPEN APPROACH, SHOWING GAUGE ARCH, MADE OF CUTTING EDGES OF SHIELD

TUNNEL WITH TWO ROWS OF LIGHTS IN USE

VIEW OF SHAFT

Pumping Plant. A pumping plant consisting of three 15 H. P. electric pumps, is located in a small house on the level of the roadway in Shaft No. 3. The pumps discharge not into the Thames, but into a sewer. As the leakage in this tunnel is small, one pump operated two hours per day is generally sufficient, and only occasionally are all three pumps used.

Cleaning, Policing and Traffic Rules. The method of cleaning and policing this tunnel is exactly the same as for the Blackwall Tunnel, as are also the rules regulating traffic.

Amount of Traffic. Statistics published by the London County Council give the following traffic figures of the number of vehicles and passengers using the Rotherhithe Tunnel since its opening:

Year	Passengers	Vehicles
1909	2,389,552	946,398
1910	2,289,820	841,542
1911	2,276,276	896,629
1912	2,256,800	973,300
1913	2,360,067	937,946

The London Traffic Branch of the Board of Trade publish the following statistics of traffic in the Rotherhithe Tunnel for an average day in 1913 and in 1914 between the hours of 8 A. M. and 8 P. M.

			1913	1914
Trade Vehicles.				
1 horse		fast	770.	543.
		slow	595.	709.
2 horses or more,				
		fast	238.	122.
		slow	307.	441.
Motor,		fast	56.	78.
		slow	109.	108.
		Total	2075.	2001.
Passenger Vehicles.				
Trams—electric				
Omnibuses,	horse			
	motor		2.	
Cabs,	horse		2.	1.
	motor		7.	8.
Carriages,	horse		19.	8.
	motor		19.	22.
		Total	49.	39.
Total horse and motor vehicles			2124.	2040.
Barrows			35.	24.
Cycles—ordinary			314.	330.
motor			1.	1.
Total traffic both ways			2474.	2395.

NUMERICAL COMPARISON OF HORSE AND MOTOR VEHICLES

	1913 %	1914 %
Percentage of horse vehicles in trade vehicles	92.	91.
Percentage of horse vehicles in passenger vehicles	43.	23.
Percentage of horse vehicles in total horse and motor vehicles	91.	89.
Percentage of trade vehicles in total (excluding cycles and barrows)	98.	98.

Operating Staff. The staff of the Rotherhithe is similar to that of the Blackwall Tunnel already described, with the addition of one more orderly boy.

Operating Cost. The approximate annual cost of operating the Rotherhithe Tunnel is as follows:

Salaries and wages	£1900
Removal of road sweepings, sprinkling roadway, supplying 300 yards of gravel and 20 yards of sand for gradients in winter	330
Water for cleaning	120
Electricity for lighting	550
Electricity for pumping	15
Supplies including lamp renewals	300
Rates	100
	£2915

In addition to this amount, the London County Council charge about £1,000 annually to this tunnel to cover engineering and general administration expense.

Comparison of River Thames Crossings with the Ferries over the Hudson River:

While the most urgent needs for additional facilities for crossing the Thames were satisfied by the construction of the above described tunnels, even with these new highways, the Thames crossings are considerably further apart than the ferries over the Hudson River. The Tower Bridge is about one-half mile below London Bridge; below it, one and three-quarters miles is the Rotherhithe Tunnel; below it, the Blackwall Tunnel is distant about four miles by river, but because of a loop in the river, only about two miles by road on the north side, and nearly five miles on the south side; below the Blackwall Tunnel, distant about three and one-quarter miles, is the Woolwich Free Ferry. Five crossings for vehicles in nine and one-half miles by river, seven and one-half miles by road on the north side, and ten and one-half miles on the south side. An average distance of about two miles apart by river.

On the New Jersey side of the Hudson River, there are eight ferry points between the Central Railroad Ferries and the West Shore Ferries, inclusive, a distance of about five miles by river. An average distance apart of eight-tenths of a mile. These eight ferry points are the termini of twelve ferries. On the New York side of the Hudson River, there are also eight ferry points from Cortlandt Street to Forty-second Street, inclusive, located at an average distance apart of only about one-half mile. These eight ferry points are the termini of thirteen ferries.

Comparison of Vehicular Traffic
River Thames and Hudson River:

For the year 1912 the traffic over the Thames free crossings was as follows:

London Bridge	5,093,900 vehicles
Tower Bridge	3,860,500 "
Rotherhithe Tunnel	973,300 "
Blackwall Tunnel	736,500 "
Woolwich Ferry	855,700 "
Total	11,519,900 "

These figures include a very large number of cycles and delivery barrows, amounting to at least 20% of the reported vehicles.

For the year 1913 the traffic over the Hudson River from the Central Railroad Ferries to the West Shore Ferries, inclusive, amounted to 5,761,685 vehicles, of which 802,355 vehicles, the largest number transported by any one ferry, were carried by the Desbrosses Street Ferry.

It is a singular coincidence that eliminating cycles and barrows from the London figures, approximately one million vehicles per year per mile cross both the Thames and Hudson Rivers.

General Impressions of Thames River Tunnels. The observation of the Thames River Tunnels developed the general facts outlined above, and created a very favorable impression as to the practicability of such highways.

Both tunnels are well designed and constructed, conveniently located and efficiently operated, but very badly ventilated.

Impressions of Traffic Operation. The Thames River tunnels are extensively used by all kinds of vehicles, operating at a variety of speeds without congestion, in a roadway sixteen feet wide between curbs. This is possible because of the general street regulation limiting heavy vehicles to a maximum width of 7 feet 6 inches between projecting points. Two vehicles of this width passing in the tunnel with the outside wheel of each against the curb, and each having a body overhang of six inches, have a clearance of two feet between vehicles. A clearance none too great, and perhaps insufficient, if many vehicles were of that width, but as light motor cars are limited to a width of 7 feet, 2 inches, and as the majority of vehicles are narrower, the tunnel operates with so little difficulty that most of the special tunnel regulations are not enforced. The stopping of vehicles except for unavoidable causes is distinctly prohibited by rule one, but vehicles are permitted to change tires or make other repairs within the tunnel, and these occasional stoppages have little perceptible effect on the flow of traffic. The speed regulations in rule ten are absolutely disregarded, and vehicles go through the tunnels at ordinary street speed with less difficulty than on a street with its cross traffic and pedestrians. Fast moving vehicles pass around slow moving vehicles going in the same direction, just as they would pass on any street, and with no difficulty.

During the recent study of these tunnels, roadway repairs were being made at several points, and at these points for perhaps one hundred yards, only one-half of the roadway was open to traffic. This perceptibly slowed the time of passing through the tunnel, but notwithstanding delays at these points, motor vehicles passed through from entrance to entrance in nine minutes, or at an average speed of eight miles per hour.

The policing of a tunnel under the Hudson River would perhaps require more officers for the same distance than is required by the London tunnels, for the reason that London streets are generally narrow, and traffic has been carefully trained to keep to the curb.

The London tunnels are not used to capacity, and even in the maximum hour when some 84 motor vehicles, 135 horse vehicles and 29 cycles and barrows pass through the Blackwall Tunnel, there is no congestion.

A study of traffic in these tunnels shows conclusively that a narrow tunnel roadway, properly policed, can accommodate two moving lines of vehicles, and permit the passing of vehicles going in the same direction, and that a speed can be maintained equal to, or perhaps exceeding, the speed maintained on an ordinary and much wider highway, for the reason that the flow of traffic is continuously in the same directions, with no vehicles joining or leaving the lines; no cross-traffic, and no pedestrians to be avoided.

Impressions of Ventilation. The ventilation of the London tunnels is distinctly bad, and it is quite evident that, with the increase in motor vehicles, artificial ventilation will shortly have to be provided. On certain days the air in the tunnels is reasonably fresh, while on others, with equal traffic, it is very bad, depending upon the direction of the wind, and upon atmospheric conditions.

The land sections between the open ends and the first shafts are short and generally well ventilated, as fresh air enters the open ends and blows out at the first shaft. The inner sections, failing to get fresh air in any quantity from the entrances, depend upon the ventilating shafts to exhaust the bad air, which is then replaced by partially vitiated air from the outer sections. Ordinarily the air in these sections while unpleasant to breathe and trying to the eyes, is not so thick that it interferes in any way with traffic, but on days of great humidity the air in the inner sections is so heavy with smoke and vapor that it is impossible to see an approaching vehicle one hundred feet away. Tunnel employes work continuously in this atmosphere with no apparent ill effects, and it is said that the only case of gas poisoning or illness ever reported was that of a policeman who claimed to have been slightly overcome a few months ago. Investigation, however, developed the fact that his illness was so slight that he had not been obliged to leave his post, and was perhaps due to some other cause.

The fact that there have been no serious prostrations, notwithstanding the passage of as many as 84 motor vehicles per hour through twelve hundred feet of practically unventilated tunnel, indicates that, with proper artificial ventilation, a much larger number of motor vehicles can pass in safety.

Respectfully submitted,

PERCY INGALLS.

Concurred in:
H. C. DONECKER.

EXHIBIT 7.

REPORT ON THE FEASIBILITY AND COST

OF A

PROPOSED VEHICULAR TUNNEL UNDER THE

HUDSON RIVER

MADE TO THE PRESIDENT OF

PUBLIC SERVICE CORPORATION OF NEW JERSEY.

By:
  William H. Burr,
  Ralph Modjeski,
  Daniel E. Moran,
   Board of Consulting Engineers.

Public Service Railway Company

29 EXCHANGE PLACE

Jersey City, N. J., January 30, 1917.

Mr. Thomas N. McCarter, President,
Public Service Corporation of New Jersey,
Newark, N. J.

Dear Sir:—

On July 15th, 1916, Mr. Walton Clark and Mr. Percy Ingalls, acting as a Committee of the Board of Direction of the Public Service Corporation of New Jersey, advised the Chairman of this Board of the purpose of your company to make certain investigations as to the feasibility and cost of a tunnel adapted to vehicular traffic under the Hudson River between Canal Street, New York City, and Twelfth Street, Jersey City, under the direction and supervision of a board of three consulting engineers. As a result of that conference, Messrs. Daniel E. Moran and William H. Burr of New York City, and Mr. Ralph Modjeski of Chicago and New York City were tentatively named for such a board. As Messrs. Moran and Modjeski were absent from the city for a succeeding fortnight it was not possible to secure their acceptances until the latter part of July. Immediately on their return the Board as named met at 29 Exchange Place, Jersey City, for its first session on August 8th, 1916, and since that time its members have been continuously engaged in the work for which the Consulting Board was created.

The line of the proposed tunnel is essentially that selected by the Interstate Bridge and Tunnel Commissions of the States of New Jersey and New York. As this is the first vehicular tunnel proposed to provide accommodation for the traffic seeking the City of New York from the adjoining part of the State of New Jersey, it is essential that the location should be such as to induce the greatest possible traffic of vehicles through it and to stimulate new traffic of the same character. Investigations made by this Board and by members of your own organization, under the direction of Mr. Percy Ingalls, Secretary, to which more extended reference will be made at another place in this report, indicate conclusively that the location selected fulfills these requirements better than any other.

Plate No. 2 shows the general plan or layout of the entire tunnel line from Canal and Varick Streets, New York City, to Twelfth and Grove Streets, Jersey City, making a total length of 9,409.19 feet from portal to portal. The lengths of the principal parts of the tunnel are as follows:

Total length, portal to portal	9,409.19 ft.
Between bulkhead lines	5,495.68 ft.
" pierhead lines	3,724.92 ft.
From New York tunnel portal to bulkhead line	1,441.00 ft.
" New Jersey " " " " "	2,472,51 ft.

Plate No. 1 shows the profile of the river on this line with the maximum depth at low water of about 55 ft. immediately in front of the New York pierhead line. On the Jersey City side the water is much shallower, but the War Department contemplates the excavation of a channel 40 ft. deep along the New Jersey side of the river.

Office and field organizations were at once created through the courtesy and aid of Mr. Martin Schreiber, Chief Engineer of your Company, utilizing members of your force in making the necessary triangulation and other surveys, performing the office work at 29 Exchange Place, Jersey City, digesting the results of field operations, making plans and estimates, and for other similar purposes necessary to attain the results set forth in this report.

Immediately after the organization of the Consulting Board suitable specifications were prepared on which bids were asked for wash and core borings carried down to and into rock along the proposed tunnel line and for the driving of timber test piles along the same location in the river between the bulkheads on either shore, these piles to be driven to the greatest depth attainable.

The contract for making the wash and core borings was awarded to Messrs. Sprague & Henwood, of Scranton, Pa., and the test pile driving to the Stillman-Delehanty-Ferris Company, of Jersey City, both of whom completed their operations effectively and within reasonable time. The complete records of all these investigations are preserved and on file in the office occupied by the Board at 29 Exchange Place, Jersey City. The number of borings and test piles driven together with the main features of the results are shown on Plate No. 1 appended to this report.

These borings and test piles give a complete and reliable record of the character and depths of the materials to be excavated or otherwise dealt with throughout the entire construction, and the data governing the use of foundation piles and the construction of other types of foundations.

The successful completion of this part of the undertaking yields the first complete and correct rock profile under the Hudson River adjacent to Manhattan Island. This profile is shown on Plates Nos. 1 and 2.

Information including all technical data disclosed by these investigations have enabled the Consulting Board to determine general plans covering the main features of the project and full estimates demonstrating the feasibility of the undertaking and its reasonable cost.

The first important consideration affecting the design of this work is the least depth below the surface of the water at which the river section of the tunnel may be placed. Prior to the inception of this work the least permissable depth below low water of the top of a tunnel structure under any of the waters of the Harbor of New York had never been determined.

In the early part of September the New Jersey Interstate Bridge and Tunnel Commission made application to the Secretary of War to fix that minimum depth which, after careful consideration by the New York Harbor

Board of Engineer Officers of the Army was placed 50 ft. below M. L. W. between the pierhead lines. The elevation of the top of this proposed tunnel must, therefore, satisfy that regulation of the War Department.

No conditions were prescribed for those parts of the tunnel between the pierhead and bulkhead lines on either side of the river. On the Manhattan side the power of regulating this depth is vested in the City of New York and in the owners of the water front on the Jersey City side. The City of New York has no fixed regulations regarding the depth of such a structure below the surface of the water at the bulkhead line, but the tops of the subway tunnels under the East River are less than 30 ft. below low water at the bulkheads and have given some trouble in connection with dredging and other operations required for the maintenance of the bulkhead structure or for the berthing of vessels. The Board has considered it best to fix this depth at 33 ft. below low water at the Canal Street bulkhead on the Hudson River. On the Jersey City side that depth has been taken as 30 ft. On both sides of the river the location of the tunnel is in the central part of the slip, so that during construction no injury may be done to adjoining piers and the least possible inconvenience to shipping be caused.

The maximum grades on the two approaches are 3.85% for the Canal Street approach and 4.55% for the Twelfth Street approach in Jersey City, both being for short distances only, the prevailing grades being 3.16% and 2.21% respectively.

The project submttted to the Consulting Board included the design of a vehicular tunnel for two lines of traffic in opposite directions, with provision for proper lateral and vertical clearances and a complete system of effective ventilation, inasmuch as power driven motor trucks or other vehicles will constitute an increasing part of the total traffic and eventually become nearly, if not the entire traffic.

A full consideration of the problem of ventilating the tunnel with sufficient power and effective appliances to accomplish that purpose will be given in a later part of this report, after a discussion of the tunnel structure.

As the river section of the tunnel is to be placed with its top not more than 50 ft. below low water, it is imperative, since the maximum depth of the water in the river is 55 ft., to provide a foundation for this part of the structure of sufficient carrying capacity to give it adequate support under all exigencies. Plate No. 1 showing the profile of the river crossing indicates the necessity of using a pile foundation as the material at no greater depth than the bottom of the tunnel at some points was found to be of silt or mud, too soft to be depended upon for the support of heavy loads as disclosed by the test piles and by the wash borings. These examinations showed a nearly uniform quality of silt and mud at the elevation of the bottom of the tunnel, practically throughout the river section except for a distance of about 1,200 ft. running from a point about 600 ft. in front of the New York pierhead line to a point half way between the same pierhead line and the adjacent bulkhead where some rock excavation will be necessary. It is entirely feasible, therefore, to dredge a trench about 40 ft. wide at the bottom and about 80 ft. below low water, except for the small amount of rock excavation already indicated to be done in compressed air. Timber piles may readily be driven and cut off accurately at the proper elevation, which with the bottom formed in the excavated rock will afford a suitable support for the tunnel structure between bulkhead lines. Outside of the bulkhead lines the approach tunnels on land may be constructed within lines of either timber or steel sheet piles by the usual procedures.

The dredged trench crossing the river, in the bottom of which foundation piles are to be driven, must not be kept open longer than necessary for the purposes of construction, as the tidal currents will tend to refill it. Sections of suitable length must, therefore, be opened progressively ahead of the tunnel construction, followed by the immediate driving and cutting off of the piles and the construction and putting in place of the tunnel sections. For the same reason comparatively flat slopes must be assumed for the dredged trench, although the material is probably solid enough to stand on steeper slopes in some parts of the river bed. It may even be advisable to hold back parts of the slopes by sheet piles, so as to reduce the dredged volume. The Board has considered it advisable, in computing the total volume of excavation, to assume the trench to be dredged to slopes of one vertical to three horizontal down to the bottom taken to be 40 ft. wide. The total dredged volume between the pierhead lines is 810,000 cu. yds.

The greatest depth reached in driving the test piles was 133 ft. below low water, and in this case, as in all the deep test pile driving, heavy spliced piles were employed. While these piles were not all driven to absolute refusal, they were driven until the penetration was so small as to be substantially refusal. It is probable, therefore, that piles 40 ft. to 70 ft. long will be required for the tunnel foundation. As the tunnel tube is to be constructed of definite dimensions and with accurate alinement and level, it is imperative that the foundation piles shall be driven not only solidly to secure adequate supporting capacity, but also with accuracy as to position and as to elevation at which they are to be cut off. The Consulting Board has, therefore, made careful studies of at least three methods of accomplishing this part of the work, the plans for which, having been sufficiently developed to show their complete practicability and effectiveness, are on file in the office of the Board. These procedures show conclusively that the foundation piles may be placed and cut off to accurate line and level so as to receive directly upon them the tunnel sections in the river, at the elevation of 78.75 ft. below low water.

The best form of tunnel section for the accommodation of the traffic passing through it has received an extended study by the Consulting Board. Obviously, the dimensions of the cross section must be sufficient and suitable to receive and pass freely while going in opposite directions, the largest vehicles permitted to be used. In the study of this part of the project the Consulting Board has availed itself of all information yielded by experience with large moving vans and other similar vehicles in the streets of New York City and the neighboring country, also of such information as the Secretary of your

Company, Mr. Percy Ingalls, has obtained in the investigation of traffic likely to seek the tunnel and, finally, investigations as to the largest vehicles used in street traffic in Chicago and in some States like New Jersey, where the subject of limiting the greatest dimensions of street vehicles has been actively agitated within the past year or year and a half. After mature deliberation and many conferences with Secretary Ingalls and Chief Engineer Schreiber of your Company, the Board recommends that the vehicle of greatest dimensions to use the tunnel be taken as having a width of 8 ft. and a maximum height of 12 ft. Two such vehicles may be so placed as to give a clearance of 3 ft. 6 in. between them, and an open space of 1 ft. 10½ in. between the wall of the tunnel and the adjacent vehicle on one side and 3 ft. 10½ in. clear space between the other wall of the tunnel and the other vehicle, and there will be a clear space of 12 in. above their tops. This Board believes, therefore, that ample provision has been made for convenient operation, maintenance and safety of laborers at all points of the tunnel at any time. At the same time the 3 ft. 10½ in. clearance will give sufficient sidewalk accommodation for people to walk out of or through the tunnel to meet any emergency of a block or accident to vehicles in the tunnel.

Plate No. 4 shows the cross section of the tunnel with sections of these vehicles and their maximum dimensions with clearances, as well as the sidewalks raised 12 in. above the floor level. The faces of the sidewalks, or curbs, are placed 17 ft. apart. These dimensions, it will be seen, make a space available for traffic in the tunnel 25 ft. wide by 13 ft. high over all. The Consulting Board recommends this section as suitable and sufficient for the purposes of the tunnel.

Plate No. 4 shows the cross section adapted to the use of reinforced concrete, i. e., it is an arch section in which there is but little bending or flexure, the water pressure on all sides subjecting the material chiefly to compression in that part of the section above the floor; it is the arch adapted to sustain to the best advantage the varying pressure of the water on the tube, and is known as a "hydrostatic arch." The lower part of the section is shaped as shown, so as to be well adapted to rest upon the tops of the piles as cut off. The minimum thickness of the ring is 4 ft., and the longitudinal and transverse steel reinforcing rods are placed near the exterior and interior surfaces as shown in Plate No. 4. For each linear foot of this type of tunnel there are 16 cu. yds. of concrete and 2,000 lbs. of reinforcing steel. Under the worst conditions of loading assumed for the tube, the maximum compression in the concrete does not exceed 500 lbs. per square inch, while the maximum tension in the steel reinforcement does not exceed 16,000 lbs. per square inch. Plate No. 4 shows how the vehicular spaces are placed in this form of section. That plate also shows the cross section of the roadway floor to be used with exhaust ducts for ventilation below it, and the ducts for the introduction of fresh air in the tops of the tunnel over the line of clearance. There are also side spaces of the tunnel available for additional ducts, or for electric or other cables or for similar purposes. It will be observed that the interior curve of the cross section is somewhat similar to the ellipse with major axis horizontal. The total height of this section is 28 ft. 4 in. and the total width 36 ft. 5 in.

Plate No. 5 shows a cross section of the second type of tube developed for the purposes of this report. The top and bottom parts are horizontal and are joined with curved sides so as to make the total width 46 ft. exclusive of the timber forms shown. There is precisely the same space for vehicular traffic as in the former section. Space is provided for air ducts at the side, thus permitting a reduction in the height of the section. The internal steel shell provides an inner form for the concrete and a watertight lining.

This section requires about 6 ft. less depth of excavation than the other, with a corresponding decrease in the amount of dredging, i. e., the minimum depth of excavation whatever may be the form of that section, but the employment of more steel and a correspondingly greater cost of tube.

The flat top and bottom of this section are subjected to heavy bending by the external water pressure, and steel columns are required to maintain the desired separation of the roof and floor without producing excessive bending of the curved sides or ends. For each linear foot of this type of tube there are 17.2 cu. yds. of concrete and 6,880 lbs. of steel. The steel is designed to carry the load or pressure of the water without being subjected to a greater tensile stress than 16,000 lbs. per square inch, with a reduction below that intensity for steel in compression depending upon the length of the compressed piece.

It will be observed that the steel frame section requires 1.2 cu. yds. more of concrete and 4,880 lbs. more of steel per linear foot than the reinforced concrete tube. The pile foundation is the same in number of piles for each tube, the greater width of the latter type requiring only a little wider spacing of the piles in each bent. This form of section is used only in the two approaches where the clearances are limited, as at the two bulkheads.

Each tunnel section may be submitted to such waterproofing treatment as may be desired. This Board recommends that the exterior form planking or lagging have its interior surface coated with waterproofing material, and that it be attached to the concrete of the section by suitable metal anchors. This Board also recommends that the interior surface of the tunnel be suitably roughened to receive a substantial coating of white Portland waterproof cement mortar for the exposed parts and with ordinary waterproof Portland cement mortar for other parts, all thoroughly worked to a smooth surface. This will not only form a waterproof coating, but the white cement will give a light and attractive finish.

This method of tunnel building contemplates the complete construction of the tunnel tube in sections of suitable length afloat or on launching ways at some convenient location. After closing the ends of these sections with timber bulkheads and towing them to the tunnel location they may be sunk accurately and safely to place by means of proper appliances, supplemented with sufficient power to control completely at all times the necessary operations. Quite similar procedures have been employed successfully in the construction of the original subway tunnel under the Harlem River and of the Detroit Tunnel and, finally, of the new subway tunnel recently constructed under the Harlem River for the Lexington Avenue Subway. When the ends of the tunnel section are closed by timber bulkheads, the tube may be floated or it may require the temporary attachment of suitable air cylinders to give it requisite flotation; in any event the actual lifting power is only a small part of the weight of the tunnel section, in fact, so much only as may be necessary to control it as a floating body. During the sinking of a tunnel section enough water is admitted to it or to the air cylinders to be just sufficient to permit the sinking of the tunnel section properly controlled until it reaches its permanent resting place.

Power scows with derricks and other requisite appliances must be fitted to perform effectively all necessary operations at all stages of the work of sinking after having been firmly anchored in their proper positions by the use of spuds as well as anchors. The maximum velocity of water to be encountered in the Hudson River on the location of this tunnel does not exceed about 3 miles per hour, whereas in the construction of the Detroit Tunnel a current of $3\frac{1}{2}$ miles per hour was encountered and without the alternating stages of dead water at high and low tide. Doubtless, advantage would be taken of the quiet waters of the ebb and flood tides in the construction of this work. The Consulting Board has made a careful study of this feature of the project under consideration, and are clear in their judgment as to the practicability of these procedures, in view of what has already been successfully accomplished in other similar works.

This Board has given full consideration both to the design of the ends of the separate tunnel sections and to the operations required for effective and safe completion of the joints in the finished tunnel tube. There are on file in the office of the Board, studies and plans sufficiently developed to show practicable methods for successfully accomplishing this purpose and demonstrating the complete feasibility of this feature of the proposed tunnel construction.

Doubtless, in the actual work of building the tunnel, the contractor would have suggestions of value to make in this connection worthy of careful consideration and perhaps adoption.

The plans and procedures already prescribed apply obviously to the main or river part of the tunnel between the pierhead lines. For a distance of about 600 ft. outside of the New York pierhead line and for about the same distance back of that line shallow rock excavation is required, and no piles can be driven in that vicinity. For this part of the work and for other locations where dredging cannot be done without injury to adjoining structures, the pneumatic process or open dredging or a combination of that process and open dredging will be used. By these procedures the rock can be excavated so as to place the tunnel tube directly upon it as a foundation by methods commonly employed under such conditions.

Again, it is obviously impracticable even with care to excavate a trench with low side slopes between pierhead and bulkhead lines without the destruction of adjoining piers, necessitating the reconstruction of these piers and the payment of damages for their non-use during the period of construction. It is, therefore, necessary to resort to some method of procedure which will leave the adjoining piers undisturbed, although the slip between those piers may not be used for commercial purposes during construction. These observations apply to both sides of the river. The Board has made complete studies with plans and estimate of cost for the construction of these parts of the tunnel by the use of pneumatic or open dredging caissons. In the use of the pneumatic caisson method the working chamber may be so constructed as to form the top and sides of the tunnel tube, leaving the bottom of the tube to be built in the pneumatic working chamber after reaching the required depth. The Board has based its estimate of cost on the use of the pneumatic process, although both methods have been shown to be entirely feasible by existing successful construction.

In the case of the open dredging caissons being used, a substantial portion of the tunnel tube may be built in the caisson before sinking and the remaining portions completed after sinking or the entire tunnel section within the limits of the caisson may be built after sinking, a floor of concrete deposited through water having been previously put in place.

The construction of the tunnel obviously will have to be carried through each bulkhead, necessitating the removal and reconstruction of a short piece of the bulkhead wall on either side of the river.

The studies and plans for the construction of these and other parts of the tunnel are on file in the office of the Board and are available whenever they may be needed.

The two land approaches extending from Canal and Varick Streets to the land side of the Canal Street bulkhead in New York City, and from Twelfth and Grove Streets to the back of the Twelfth Street bulkhead in Jersey City are designed as usual tunnels in earth, constructed in the open between suitable lines of heavy timber or steel sheet piling similar to parts of the subway construction in New York City. Although much of these approaches would be built in excavation considerably below water level, the requisite operations present no unusual features of engineering construction. After the completion of the tunnel tube the space between the two lines of sheet piling and above the tube would obviously be backfilled and paved wherever the street surface may have been removed.

As already indicated, the river section of the tunnel tube has been so modified as to be advantageously adapted to either the pneumatic or open dredging processes or to the open excavation work for the two land approaches, the purpose being in all cases to secure the most economical and effective section. The requisite traffic space already fully described for the river section of the tunnel will be maintained the same throughout the entire length of the tunnel from portal to portal. Furthermore, ducts or other features of the work required for the effective ventilation of all parts of the tunnel will, of course, be provided, whatever adaptation of the river section might be necessary at any point.

Plans accompanying this report show fully the sections and their features for all parts of the work, designed to meet the various conditions and requirements which have been considered.

Inasmuch as a considerable percentage of the vehicles using the proposed tunnel will use gasoline engines as their motive power, and ultimately nearly all vehicles may be of that type, it is essential for the convenient and safe operation of traffic that a sufficient and effective system of ventilation be provided. Although much has already been done in the ventilation of railway and subway tunnels and in the ventilation of mines in which gasoline locomotives are used, there has yet been no occasion for a complete ventilation of a traffic tunnel in which the air is vitiated by the gases of combustion from gasoline motors. In some steam railway cases over 600,000 cu. ft. of fresh air per minute have been driven into a tunnel for the purpose of keeping the smoke and gases of combustion of a locomotive ahead of it, and so prevent passengers and train crews from being immersed in them. The problem of a railway tunnel, however, is quite different from that of a traffic tunnel in which vehicles driven by gasoline motors are used. In the railway tunnel all smoke and gases of combustion are produced at one, two or three points only, while in the proposed traffic tunnel every gasoline motor driven vehicle is the center of production of vitiating gases. In conditions of congested traffic it must be assumed that the gasoline motor vehicles produce a continuous line with short head room between, extending throughout the greater part or all of the tunnel, for traffic in both directions. It becomes necessary then to determine some definite basis for the control of the vitiated air in the tunnel and the supply of a corresponding amount of fresh air.

The precise degree of vitiation of the air of a vehicular tunnel before it becomes unsafe to breathe has not yet been determined. Mr. Percy Ingalls, Secretary, found that there is at present no artificial ventilation in the Rotherhithe or Blackwall Tunnels under the River Thames in London, and that both are subjected to a rather heavy traffic in motor driven vehicles; but he also learned that the air in these tunnels has now become so vitiated that it appears probable that resort must soon be made to artificial ventilation.

Recent investigations in the ventilation of buildings have shown that any amount of carbon dioxide ordinarily generated in places where a large number of people congregate is not materially disagreeable or otherwise objectionable, provided the vitated atmosphere is kept in motion. On the other hand, other recent investigations have shown carbon monoxide to be a dangerous element in the products of combustion, and that one of the principal functions of the fresh air introduced for ventilating purposes, is a dilution of that gas to a point where its presence is immaterial. Some investigators have concluded from their tests that the carbon monoxide should be diluted to the extent of 1,000 parts of fresh air to 1 part of the monoxide. Some investigations carried on by the Bureau of Mines in the Department of the Interior have apparently given some support to that view of the matter, but it has not yet been clearly established that a much less dilution will not accomplish all that is desired.

The principal products of combustion in gasoline driven motors are carbon monoxide, carbon dioxide and smoke, due not only to the combustion of the gasoline, but also to the lubricating oil in the cylinders.

In its treatment of the ventilation of this tunnel the Board has placed the exhaust ducts under the floor and the fresh air ducts at the top of the tunnel, as there are some material advantages in that arrangement. The power required, however, and the cost of ventilation will not be affected if it should be found advisable to reverse the relative positions of the ducts, nor would any of the conclusions reached be modified.

After having given extended consideration to available data regarding the most recent and complete ventilation experiences, with the aid of Mr. Jackes of your organization and others, this Board recommends the construction of a shaft 34 ft. interior diameter and 50 ft. high at either end of the river section of this unnnel, about 5,500 ft. apart, for the introduction of fresh air by natural flowage induced by the exhaustion of the vitiated air, but supplemented by an additional volume from each end to be blown in by suitable fans through ducts of proper size built in the top of the tunnel over the clear vehicular way, this latter fresh air to be not less in volume than the amount brought in through the shafts. It is clear that the flow of fresh air downward through these two shafts would make the air at and near their bottoms nearly as fresh as the outside air, but that as the air flows through the tunnel toward the center it will become increasingly vitiated, the greatest vitiation being in the vicinity of the central point between the two shafts. It appears, therefore, that the fresh air brought in through the ducts placed in the top of the tunnel should be discharged within the central zone of this section of the tunnel, perhaps, for illustration, within 500 ft. each way from the center of the 5,500 ft. length. It is the judgment of the Board that the exhaust ducts should be placed in the bottom of the tunnel underneath the roadway floor; also that both the fans blowing in the fresh air and those used in exhausting the vitiated air under the roadway floor should be placed in suitable chambers at the two shafts on either side of the river. The area of the cross section of the fresh air ducts in the top of the tunnel is about 52 sq. ft., while the area of the cross section of the exhaust ducts under the roadway floor is about 70 sq. ft., including the empty spaces under the two narrow sidewalks. The orifices leading into the exhaust ducts will be distributed uniformly throughout the entire length of the river section of tunnel, either along the gutter or along the center lines of the traffic moving in the two directions or both. These exhaust openings are to be adjustable, so that the most effective conditions for the withdrawal of the vitiated air may be determined by trial after completion of the tunnel. The general condition of the tunnel atmosphere would then be an inflow of fresh air from the two shafts at the ends of the river section and from the fresh air ducts in the top of the tunnel throughout the central zone concurrently with the exhaustion of the vitiated air and the products of combustion through the openings of the roadway floor leading into the exhaust ducts.

The Board's investigation of the possible traffic through the tunnel, made by the aid of the statistics of ferry traffic across the Hudson River secured by Mr. Percy Ingalls, indicates that satisfactory ventilation should be provided for 180 motor vehicles simultaneously in the 5,500 ft. length of tunnel between the shafts, which may be either in motion or, in case of a block, at rest with engines running light. This will require the expenditure of about 500 H. P. to produce a dilution of not less than 500 volumes of fresh air to 1 of the monoxide and a complete change of tunnel atmosphere about every five minutes. That operation necessitates the introduction of 360,000 cu. ft. of fresh air per minute, and will be sufficient to produce entirely satisfactory ventilation of this part of the tunnel.

The ventilation of the approach tunnels is a comparatively simple matter, for the reason that one intermediate shaft will be constructed at about the middle point of the New Jersey approach, reducing the greatest length to be ventilated at one operation to about 1,400 ft., while the New York approach is also about 1,400 ft. long and will be served by fans placed at the New York shaft.

The total power required to ventilate the entire tunnel at what may be called the peak load is 750 H. P. At all other times a much reduced expenditure of energy will be required. It is not unlikely that less than one-third of the peak load energy will be sufficient throughout much of the day and the greater part of the night.

The estimate of cost of this entire work is based upon prices existing under what may be termed ordinary or normal conditions of business. At the present time abnormal conditions of business exist and the prices of some materials used in large quantities in engineering operations are unusually high. Structural steel work manufactured and put in place commands at least double what may be considered the ordinary or normal cost and for some special purposes the price is even much higher. The price of cement is probably at least 50% above its normal cost for engineering work. Other materials have experienced a less rise in value, and the price of labor for some of the larger contracts for public work in New York City is not greatly advanced. As these abnormal conditions are not likely to hold for any extended period, the Board has thought it advisable to determine the estimate of cost on the normal or ordinary basis and then indicate about what increase would have to be made to meet the prices ruling at the date of this report.

In making this estimate the Board has availed itself of information furnished by contractors in some instances, of actual prices on which similar work has recently been awarded under public competition, of the normal and present prices for a large number of materials as furnished by the Purchasing Agent of your Corporation and of the experiences of its members in their own fields of actual work, both at present and in the past. Thorough and detailed study has been given to every feature of the work involved in the construction of this tunnel so as to reach the most reasonable actual costs. The full details of this estimate, classified and arranged so as to show what each principal part of the proposed work will cost, is on record in the office of the Board at Jersey City and is available for your examination.

The complete estimate of cost of construction of this tunnel from portal to portal, including profit to the contractor, engineering and contingencies, but not interest during construction, is $6,899,000. This sum is a reasonable price for the work under ordinary or normal business conditions. If the work were to be done at this date with the prices now ruling, it would be necessary to add about 30% or about $2,000,000 to the price named above. It is the judgment of the Board that the work could be completed within a period of two years from the actual beginning of construction.

The Board has taken no steps to determine the cost of necessary real estate as that can be done more effectively by members of your own organization familiar with real estate matters. After the requisite amount is determined it can be added to the estimated cost as given above.

The work of construction in the slip, at least on the New York side of the river, will prevent the adjoining side of the pier from being used by the tenant, necessitating an adjustment before beginning construction, not included in the estimate of cost.

A comparison of cost of this tunnel with the cost of similar work successfully done by the usual shield method in New York City is necessary in order that advantages attaching to the methods of construction set forth in this report may be properly gauged. One of the latest tunnels driven by the shield method and at the lowest contract price reached up to the present time is the East Fourteenth Street Rapid Transit Tunnel, consisting of two cast iron tubes, each 18 ft. in diameter, lined with concrete 15 in. thick. This double tube has a length of 7,089 ft., as indicated by the contract plans, "Route No. 8, Section No. 3." The contract price is $6,639,023.50, making an average cost for the two tubes of $937.00 per linear foot. There are of course no portals as this tunnel is simply a part of the subway between stations.

It is approximately correct, at least, to assume that the costs of two tunnels of different areas of cross section built by the same process and under nearly the same general conditions will be about as the areas of those cross sections. The cross sectional area of the two Fourteenth Street tubes is 533 sq. ft., whereas the area of an exterior circular cross section, 33 ft. in diameter, giving the requisite vehicular clearances provided for this tunnel, with a total thickness of wall of 2 ft. 6 in., would be 855 sq. ft. If such a vehicular tunnel should be built by the shield method, it is fair to assume in this comparison that its cost would reach nearly ($\frac{855}{533} = 1.6$) $\times$ $937.00 or $1,499.00 per linear foot, whereas the full estimate of cost, as given in this report, of that part of the vehicular tunnel, designed by this Board, lying between bulkhead walls with a length of about 5,600 ft. is about $765 per linear foot. Again, as the area of the exterior cross section of this vehicular tunnel is 877 sq. ft., the cost of its most expensive part per linear foot, with an area of cross section about two-thirds more than that of the East River double tube tunnel, is less than 82% of that for the shield driven tunnel.

Moreover, there is grave doubt whether a metal tube 33 ft. in diameter should not be of steel castings rather than cast iron, which would still further increase the cost of the shield driven tunnel. The excessively large shield required for a 33 ft. tube would be a source of both enhanced difficulties and cost in consequence of its size and the great differences in depth below the water surface of its highest and lowest parts. Finally, there would be a serious disadvantage due to a much greater depth of the roadway below water, necessitating either steeper grades for the approaches or correspondingly greater lengths.

This Board has given attention to two possible alternative New York approaches, either one to take the place of the proposed Canal Street approach. One of these is along West Street and the other along Spring Street and either one may take the place of the Canal Street approach without material change in the cost of construction, the lengths being substantially the same.

If there should be a double approach on West Street, one from the north and one from the south, each providing two way traffic, there would be a large increase in the cost of construction. At the point of branching near to, but east of the bulkhead, a high and low grade crossing would have to be provided to save a serious restriction of tunnel capacity. This would be a costly feature to construct. In fact, the excessive additional cost of this double, i. e., north and south approach on West Street, would probably more than counterbalance any advantages of a double entrance.

While the estimate of cost covers the ventilating plant with its power installation and the electric lighting plant, the annual cost for power to operate them is not included, but it may be taken as follows, as shown by reference to Appendix No. 8:

Annual cost for power for ventilating plant	$36,185
" " " current for lighting	11,899
Total	$48,084

The capacity of the tunnel obviously will depend upon the headway between vehicles and the speed at which they may be assumed to travel. It is reasonable to assume that vehicles 60 ft. apart from center to center may safely travel at a speed of 10 miles per hour. If such an assumption be made for vehicles so placed along the two lines of traffic proceeding in opposite directions, the number of vehicles passing through the tunnel in twenty-four hours would be 42,240, or 15,417,600 in a year of 365 days. It is scarcely conceivable that such traffic could ever exist and yet with reasonable conditions of uninterrupted traffic the capacity of the tunnel may be considered sufficient for such a result. Even if the usual interruptions of minor accidents and the decrease of traffic at night should reduce the computed amount one-half there still would be a traffic of over 7,700,000 vehicles in a year.

Some traffic details resulting from the actual count of vehicles using North River ferries and bearing upon the traffic tributary to this tunnel may be found in Appendix No. 7.

Investigations bearing upon the vitiation of the air in the tunnel due to the operation of gasoline motor vehicles and upon the amount of ventilation required are being conducted in a specially constructed testing house whose transverse cross section is practically identical with the cross section of the vehicular space in the tunnel and with a length of 125 ft. at Passaic Wharf under the direction of Dr. Gellert Alleman. These tests include the determination of the vitiation of the atmosphere of the testing house by the operation of as many as eight gasoline motor vehicles both with and without ventilation. The complete report of these tests with chemical analyses and other results may be found in Appendix No. 10.

The organization of an effective force for the operation of this tunnel, including the regulation of traffic and the ventilating and electric lighting plants, is shown in Appendix No. 9. The annual cost for this force is $49,525.00, as will be seen by reference to the same Appendix.

The results of the investigations covered by this report and of the treatment of the various elements of the matters submitted to us, as set forth in the report, show conclusively that:

1. It is entirely feasible to construct a vehicular tunnel under the Hudson River between Canal Street, New York City, and Twelfth Street, Jersey City, with the top surface of the tube 50 ft. below M. L. W. and supported upon an adequate pile foundation, on the line indicated in the plans attached to this report.

2. It is entirely feasible to ventilate satisfactorily such a tunnel tube when used by gasoline motor vehicles in numbers practically equal to its capacity.

3. The total cost of construction of such a tunnel fully equipped with ventilating and electric lighting plants is $6,899,000, including contractor's profit, engineering and contingencies.

4. The annual cost of operation of the tunnel, including the force required and the power both for ventilating and lighting, is $97,609.

Respectfully submitted,

Wm. H. Burr,
Ralph Modjeski,
Daniel E. Moran.

Oversized Foldout

Oversized Foldout

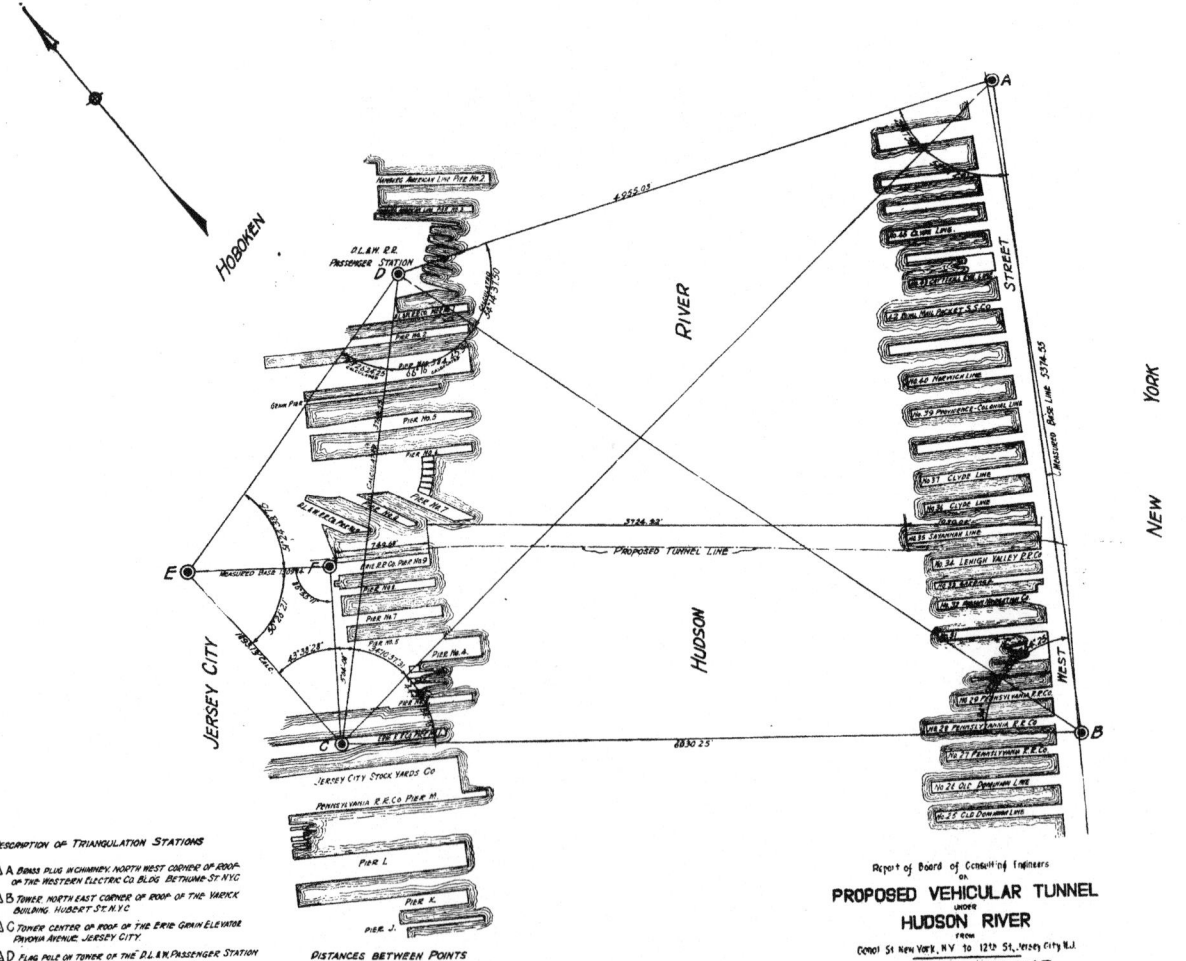

Oversized Foldout

Oversized Foldout

Oversized Foldout

APPENDIX No. 1.

PERMIT AND REGULATIONS ISSUED BY THE U. S. WAR DEPARTMENT FOR THE CONSTRUCTION OF A TUNNEL UNDER THE NORTH RIVER BETWEEN CANAL STREET, NEW YORK CITY, AND THIRTEENTH STREET, JERSEY CITY, AT THE MINIMUM PERMISSABLE DEPTH BELOW LOW WATER.

This permit and these regulations were issued in September 1916, to the New Jersey Intersate Bridge and Tunnel Commission through the U. S. Engineer's Office of the First District, New York, Colonel Harry Taylor, U. S. A. Engineer Officer. The wash borings and test pile driving in the Hudson River between the pierhead lines were performed under these regulations and under the inspection of the U. S. Engineer's Office.

PERMIT

Whereas, By Section 10 of an act of Congress, approved March 3, 1899, entitled "An act making appropriations for the construction, repair and preservation of certain public works on rivers and harbors, and for other purposes," it is provided that it shall not be lawful to build or commence the building of any wharf, pier, dolphin, boom, weir, breakwater, bulkhead, jetty, or other structures in any port, roadstead, haven, harbor, canal, navigable river, or other water of the United States, outside established harbor lines, or where no harbor lines have been established, except on plans recommended by the Chief of Enginers and authorized by the Secretary of War; and it shall not be lawful to excavate or fill, or in any manner to alter or modify the course, location, condition, or capacity of, any port, roadstead, haven, harbor, canal, lake, harbor of refuge, or inclosure within the limits of any breakwater, or of the channel of any navigable water of the United States, unless the work has been recommended by the Chief of Engineers and authorized by the Secretary of War prior to beginning the same; and

Whereas, Application has been made to the Secretary of War by the New Jersey Interstate Bridge and Tunnel Commission for authority to construct a vehicular tunnel under the Hudson River, New York and New Jersey, from about Canal Street, New York, N. Y., to Thirteenth Street, Jersey City, N. J., the plans for which have been recommended by the Chief of Engineers; now

Therefore, This is to certify that the Secretary of War hereby authorizes the said work of constructing a vehicular tunnel under the Hudson River, New York and New Jersey, from about Canal Street, Manhattan Borough, New York City to Thirteenth Street, Jersey City, N. J., in the location shown on the plans, upon the following conditions:

1. That it is to be understood that this authority does not give any property rights in real estate or material, or any excessive privileges; and that it does not authorize any injury to private property or invasion of private rights, or

any infringement of Federal, State or local laws or regulations, nor does it obviate the necessity of obtaining State assent to the work authorized. It MERELY EXPRESSES THE ASSENT OF THE FEDERAL GOVERNMENT SO FAR AS CONCERNS THE PUBLIC RIGHTS OF NAVIGATION. (See Cummings v. Chicago, 188 U. S., 410.)

2. That the work shall be subject to the supervision and approval of the Engineer Officer of the United States Army in Charge of the locality, who may temporarily suspend the work at any time if, in his judgment, the interest of navigation so require.

3. That if any pipe, wire, pile, or cable is herein authorized, it shall be placed and maintained with a clearance not less than that shown by the profile on the plan attached hereto.

4. That so far as any material is dredged in the prosecution of the work herein authorized it shall be removed evenly, and no large refuse piles shall be left. It shall be deposited to the satisfaction of the said engineer officer and in accordance with his prior permission or instructions, either on shore above high water or at such dumping ground as may be designated by him, and where he may so require, within or behind a good and substantial bulkhead or bulkheads, such as will prevent escape of the material into the waterway; and so far as the pipe, wire, or cable is laid in a trench, the formation of permanent ridges across the bed of the waterway shall be avoided and the back filling shall contain no rock and shall be so done as not to increase the cost of future dredging for navigation. If the material is to be deposited in the harbor of New York, or in its adjacent or tributary waters, or in Long Island Sound, a permit therefor must be previously obtained from the Supervisor of New York Harbor, Army Building, New York City.

5. That there shall be no unreasonable interference with navigation by the work herein authorized.

6. That if inspections or any other operations by the United States are necesssary in the interests of navigation, all expenses connected therewith shall be borne by the permittee.

7. That if future operations by the United States require an alteration in the position of the structure or work herein authorized, or if, in the opinion of the Secretary of War, it shall cause unreasonable obstruction to the free navigation of said water, the permittee will be required, upon due notice from the Secretary of War, to remove or alter the structural work or obstructions caused thereby without expense to the United States so as to render navigation reasonably free, easy, and unobstructed; and if, upon the expiration or revocation of this permit, the structure, fill, excavation, or other modification of the watercourse hereby authorized shall not be completed, the permittee, at his own expense, and to such extent and in such time and manner as the Secretary of War may require, shall remove all or any portion of the uncompleted structure or fill and restore to its former condition the navigable capacity of the watercourse. No claim shall be made against the United States on account of any such removal or alteration.

8. That there shall be installed and maintained on the work, by and at the expense of the permitee, such lights and signals as may be prescribed by the Bureau of Lighthouses, Department of Commerce.

9. That the permitee shall notify the said engineer officer at what time the work will be commenced, and as far in advance of the time of commencement as the said engineer officer may specify, and shall also notify him promptly, in writing, of the commencement of work, suspension of work, if for a period of more than one week, resumption of work, and its completion.

10. That if the structure or work herein authorized is not completed and written notice of completion is not filed with the aforesaid engineer officer on or before the 31st day of December 1921, this authorization, if not previously revoked or specifically extended, shall cease and be null and void.

11. That the permittee shall assume all legal liability for any loss or damage due to the construction, maintenance, or operation of any of the works and structures, or for loss or damage to any of the work hereby authorized; and said permittee, directly or indirectly, shall make no demand or claim of any kind against the United States or any officer or agent thereof for any loss or damage to the work or structures or to the permittee in the construction, maintenance and operation of the same, caused by any officer or agent of the United States acting under or by virtue of his authority as such; and said permittee shall not attempt in any way to prevent free use by the public of any area outside of that actually covered by the work or structure authorized.

12. That no part of the permanent structure between the pierhead lines along the New York side and along the New Jersey side, as approved by the Secretary of War, shall be above a plane situated fifty (50) feet below mean low water and all temporary structures shall be removed to the same depth.

13. That not more than   feet in width of the river, nor more than   feet in the length thereof shall be obstructed at one time by the plant and appliances, and anchors used in the work of construction.

14. That all floating plant and anchors used in the work shall display the signals and shall be marked as required by the rules and regulations approved by the Secretary of War August 18, 1916, and published in War Department form No. 46, authorized September 8, 1916. These signals shall be displayed continuously until it has been ascertained that the depth of water over all structures, except anchors placed in the river, is not less than the required depth of fifty (50) feet below mean low water, and all floating plant, appliances, and anchors have been removed from the site of the work.

15. That during the presence of the plant, appliances, and anchors, or any part thereof, at the site of the work, suitable power boats shall be stationed about one mile above the site and about one mile below the site, whose duty it shall be to warn all approaching craft of the existence and location of the obstructed area.

16. That no obstruction shall be placed in the river east of a line situated 1,000 feet west of and parallel to the pierhead line along the New York water front until the existing 40 ft. channel shall have been widened, at the expense of the permittee, to such an extent as to provide a channel with a depth of not less than 40 feet at M. L. W. and 1,000 feet in width exclusive of the space occupied by the permittee's plant for such distance upstream and downstream from the line of the proposed work as may be directed by the District Officer.

17. That the permittee shall, at his expense, cause navigation interests to be notified of the proposed obstruction by publication in at least two prominent local daily papers; by circular letter to all persons, companies, or corporations owning or operating floating plant in New York Harbor and adjacent waters so far as this may be practically possible. Since the work of construction probably will be prosecuted intermittently, the notice herein required shall be given, in each instance, a reasonable time in advance of the proposed work.

18. If during the progress of the work any plant, machinery, appliance, or material should be sunk, lost, or thrown overboard, or misplaced, which, in the opinion of the Engineer Officer of the United States Army in charge of the locality, may be dangerous to or obstruct navigation, the permittee shall recover and remove the same with the utmost dispatch.

19. That the United States shall be represented on the work by one or more inspectors appointed by the said Engineer Officer each at a salary not to exceed one hundred and twenty-five dollars ($125) per month and subsistence, or subsistence allowance of sixty cents ($0.60) per day, and five dollars ($5) per day additional for Sundays and legal holidays when work on these holidays is being carried on. Payment for all services and allowances of inspectors shall be made by the permittee through the office of the said Engineer Officer on bills submitted by said office, and as a guarantee for the proper discharge of this obligation the permittee shall deposit with the said Engineer Officer in the form of a certified check made payable to the official order of that officer, an amount sufficient to cover the cost of the inspection referred to herein and in paragraph 6 foregoing for a period of three (3) months in advance; provided that upon the completion of the work, and the final discharge of the permittee's obligation, with regard to salaries and allowances of United States Inspector and to the cost of any additional inspectors (par. 6) the full amount of the security then on hand shall be returned to the permittee, it being understood that the security, or any part thereof, shall be disbursed by the United States only in the payment of the salaries and allowances of the Inspectors and of the cost of the inspections (par. 6) on the failure of the said permittee to make payment therefor on bills rendered by the office of the said Engineer Officer.

20. That if, during the progress of the work, "blow-outs" or other accidents should occur, or be deemed likely to occur, such steps for remedy or prevention may be taken as may be approved by the said Engineer Officer.

APPENDIX No. 2.

WASH BORINGS, CORE BORINGS AND TEST PILES.

The specimens of materials obtained both in the wash and core borings were suitably bottled and boxed for preservation and were deposited on the date of this report in the office used by the Consulting Board at 29 Exchange Place, Jersey City, N. J., and are available by the Public Service Corporation of New Jersey whenever they may be desired. The following sheets and the test specimens constitute the complete data obtained from these investigations.

Specifications under which both parts of this work were done will be found below and form part of this appendix.

SPECIFICATIONS

FOR

BORINGS APPROXIMATELY ON A LINE RUNNING FROM CANAL STREET, MANHATTAN, TO TWELFTH STREET, JERSEY CITY.

Specifications for Borings Approximately on a Line Running from Canal Street, Manhattan, to Twelfth Street, Jersey City.

These borings will be mainly jet or wash borings and there will be three groups:—One on land approximately along the line of Twelfth St. or Twelfth St. extended, or in the vicinity of that street in Jersey City; the second along the line of Canal St., Manhattan, or adjacent thereto, and the third in the North River, between the first and second groups.

BORINGS ON LAND

These jet or wash borings will be made in the usual manner by means of an outer pipe or casing in short sections forced into the ground and a smaller inner pipe through which the jet of water is to be forced in order to wash out the solid material down to such depths as may be prescribed. In these borings the water may be forced down through the inner pipe, either by suitable hand or power pump.

These borings will be carried down to bed rock if required or to a depth not exceeding about 125 ft.

Provision must be made for blasting with small charges of dynamite, if necessary, in order to determine whether apparent rock encountered is a boulder or ledge rock. It is not anticipated that blasting will be needed to displace any other hard material than boulders or other rock, but if required, resort may be made to blasting to displace any material too hard to be eroded or displaced by water jet.

These borings will probably be made from 100 to 150 ft. apart along the lines indicated, but other borings off the line may be required at any points where it is desired to secure additional information regarding sub-surface materials.

The total number of these land borings on both sides of the river can scarcely be even approximately stated, but they may aggregate fifty or more.

As the borings progress an observer not supplied by the bidder will constantly be in attendance at the point of discharge from the outer pipe or casing so as to secure specimens of solid matter brought up by the water and be continuously informed of the material penetrated. Frequent specimens of the solid material taken so as to indicate each change of material, and separately washed up must be put into broad mouthed short bottles ordinarily used for such purposes, to be corked and labelled, together with such data as will identify the location and elevation from which the material has been taken. All such material specimens and other data or records taken or made in connection with these borings shall be arranged so as to be continuous in order and shall be turned over to and become the property of the Owner.

Among other data care should be taken to determine as closely as possible the sub-surface water level and the close or open character of the material penetrated.

The party doing this work shall scrupulously respect and be governed by any regulations imposed by the municipalities of New York and Jersey City. The parties making the borings will secure from the proper City official the requisite permits required for the temporary partial occupation of the streets at points where the borings are made.

The Owner will provide an Engineering Representative who will give general directions regarding the location of the borings and the conduct of the operations and who is to be afforded full opportunity at all times to inspect the work in progress and give such directions for its performance as he may deem best.

RIVER BORINGS

The borings to be made in the river will be of the same general character as those made on land and all the provisions for effective working records, specimens of material penetrated, etc., etc., on land are equally applicable to the borings made in the bed of the river.

It will be necessary to provide a suitable scow or barge, approved as to dimensions by the Board of Consulting Engineers, fitted with the requisite leads and power equipment to handle the pipes used in making the borings. Effective anchors with proper length of lines must be supplied so as to hold the scow or barge accurately and steadily in position while the work of making any borings is in progress. These provisions must be made in view of the large volume of water traffic which will constantly be passing the site of a boring. At points where the depth of the water and the character of the bottom will permit it may be necessary to use piles or spuds to hold the barge true to its position.

Inasmuch as the depth of the water in the river is great and light collisions at least are to be anticipated, the outer casing or pipe to be used must not be less than 6 in. in diameter and it may be necessary to increase that diameter if it should be found advisable. As already indicated, both the pumping and the handling of the pipes must be done by power for the borings in the river.

The depth to which these borings may be carried cannot be indicated prior to undertaking the work. The depth penetrated may be as much as 150 ft. below low water or more. Special care must be exercised in these river borings as in those on land to secure the most complete and continuous record possible regarding all material and its character, including the specimens for permanent record.

These borings will be located about 150' apart along the line indicated, but others may be required wherever it may be advisable to secure additional information.

The position of each boring in the river will be accurately located by instrumental observations and that location must be closely held while the work of boring is in progress.

It will be necessary to have a tug equipped with suitable power in constant attendance on the scow for the purpose of quick and accurate manipulation and also for the purpose of protecting the scow, as far as possible, from being struck or collided with by passing craft. The suitability of this tug, as well as the remaining plant, must be subject to the approval of the Engineer in charge of the work.

All provisions prescribed by the U. S. Engineer Officer of this District and all regulations as to lights, buoys, signals or other regulations must be scrupulously respected in this river work.

CORE BORINGS

A few core borings only, if any, will be needed, but it is desired to provide for such borings if it appears to be advisable to penetrate the ledge rock. It is anticipated that the most of these borings will be required on land along Canal Street, Manhattan, and in water opposite Canal Street; i. e., in the vicinity of Pier 42. For core borings in the water provision should be made on the scow to use the casing pipe employed for wash borings in the river so as to drill out the core inside of that pipe and below its lower end.

On shore a similar procedure can be followed if it is considered advisable. The depth of borings into rock cannot be pre-determined as it will depend upon rock elevation. If the latter is relatively high it may be necessary to take a core of 15 ft. or 20 ft. or more from the rock, but if the ledge is at a low elevation it will be necessary to penetrate it but a few feet. The diameter of the core may be anything from about one inch to two inches. In case core borings are required a careful record of the entire boring operation must be made and the entire core taken out, whether continuous or in small pieces, and placed in the usual long narrow box for permanent keeping, the depths at which the different parts of the core were taken being indicated on the box or in some other equally effective manner.

Contractors will base their bids on the foregoing specification and in accord with the following assumptions:

A Land Borings:

There will not be less than 40 borings to be made inside of the bulkhead lines of New York City and New Jersey, the 40 borings to aggregate not less than 2,000 linear feet above the depth of 125 ft.

Contractor will bid:

1. Price per foot of finished wash pipe boring to depth required not in excess of 125 ft. No allowance will be made for borings not going to the depth called for by the Engineer in charge.

2. Price per foot for additional depth if called for below the depth of 125 ft.
3. Price per sample for dry samples.
4. Price per foot for core borings in rock.

B Water Borings:

There will be not less than 20 borings in the river between bulkhead lines and the contractor may assume that the 20 borings will aggregate not less than 2,000 linear feet above the depth of 125 ft.

Contractor will bid:

1. Price per linear foot of finished boring to depth required (not in excess of 100 ft. below river bottom) from the bottom of the river. No allowance will be made for borings not going to depth called for by the Engineer in charge.
2. Price per foot for additional depth if called for below a depth of 100 ft. below river bottom.
3. Price per sample for dry samples.
4. Price per foot for core borings in rock.

SPECIFICATIONS

FOR

DRIVING TEST PILES IN THE NORTH RIVER APPROXIMATELY ON A LINE RUNNING FROM CANAL STREET, MANHATTAN, TO TWELFTH STREET, JERSEY CITY.

Test Pile Data.

No of Pile	Distance from Savannah Pier Head North or South of C.L. of Tunnel Feet	Bottom below Mean Low Water Feet	Size of Pile Dia Tip Inches	Size of Pile Dia Butt Inches	Length Feet	Length Followed Feet	Weight Pile below Hammer	Under Weight of Hammer	Under Blows of Hammer (Fall of Hammer in feet=H, given in bracket) 1st	2nd	3rd	4th	5th	6th	Last 6 Blows	Total No of Blows	Penetration under M.L.W. Feet	Total Penetration below L.W.S. Feet	Average for last 5 blows Inches	Weight of Hammer in lbs. W.	Safe bearing Capacity of Pile 2WH/S+1 lbs Free fall	Safe bearing Capacity of Pile 4WH/S+1 lbs Restrained	Penetration into River Bottom Feet	Remarks
1	445 S.W. on C.L.	15.5	7	17	80.0	53.3	28.0	9.2 (6.0)	2.4	2.7	2.3	1.5	1.8	.2 .1 .1 .1 .1 .0	142	57.3	94.5	1.2	4500	89,100	39,300	79.0	
2	429 S.W. on C.L.	13.1	6	16	82.2	53.5	35.6	11.4 (4.0)	3.5	3.5	2.0	2.5	2.1	.1 .1 .1 .1 .1 .0	120	44.0	91.0	.8	4500	60,000	48,000	77.9	
3	411 S.W. 1.5 N.	13.1	6	16	82.2	52.0	35.0	10.2 (4.5)(3.8)	1.7	2.5	3.0	1.8	0 (3) .1 .1 .0 .1 .0	165	51.4	96.6	.4	4500	77,100	61,700	83.5	Pile broke 4.2 from tip
4	411 S.W. on C.L.	11.1	7	15	81.8	53.7	32.5	14.6 (3.0)	3.4	3.2	2.9	2.9	2.0	.2 .1 .2 .2 .2 .0	213	79.8	127.2	1.8	4500	38,600	30,900	116.1	
5	389 S.W. on C.L.	14.6	7	18	80.7	52.0	27.8	18.0 (6)	1.6	1.8	1.8	1.3	1.9	.2 .1 .1 .2 .1 .0	289	81.7	127.5	1.2	4500	45,000	36,000	112.9	
6	372 S.W. 1.5 S.	6.5	8	16	86.7	53.2	27.3	10.0 (6)	2.4	1.7	1.3	2.8 (2)	2.0	.2 (4) .1 .1 .2 .1 .1	338	92.0	129.3	1.2	3800	62,200	49,800	122.8	
7	372 S.W. 1.5 N.	18.4	7	18	80.7	45.0	31.4	12.0 (2.0)	2.2	2.1	2.0	1.7	1.5	.2 (3) .2 .2 .1 .1 .1	214	74.8	118.2	1.8	3800	48,800	39,100	94.8	This pile broke when pulled
8	239 S.W. 1.5 N.	32.5	8	16	120.6	42.7	66.3	4.2 (4) .3 .11 .4 .5 .7						.1 (4) .2 .1 .1 .1 .1	207	62.5	133.0	1.8	4500	38,600	30,900	100.5	was blasted
9	211 S.W. 1.5 N.	34.6	8	16	127.0	24.5	69.2	6.0 (4) 2.5 .7 1.4 (2) 1.4 .8						.1 (4) .2 .2 .1 .1 .1	151	56.1	131.3	2.0	3800	45,600	36,500	96.7	
10	211 S.W. 1.5 S.	34.2	8	16	127.0	26.8	67.7	2.2 2.4 (4) 1.5 .1 1.6 (2) 1.22						.2 (3) .2 .2 .1 .1 .1	172	58.2	128.1	1.6	3800	35,100	28,100	93.9	
11	193 S.W. 1.5 N.	35.0	8	17	117.5	24.5	61.7	8.6 (8) 1.3 1.0 1.3 1.4 1.1						.1 (4) .1 .1 .0 .1 .2	210	62.9	133.2	1.8	"	48,800	39,100	98.2	
12	196 S.W. 1.5 S.	35.0	8	17	115.5	24.5	60.0	5.4 (8) .5 .7 .8 .8 .6						.1 (4) .1 .2 .0 .2 .0	214	61.4	120.0	1.4	"	38,000	30,400	92.0	
13	170 S.W. 1.5 N.	39.0	8	17	118.5	24.5	62.3	.6 .7 (8) 2.0 .1 .3 .8 1.3						.1 (4) .1 .0 .0 .1 .1	230	64.2	127.1	.8	"	76,000	60,800	98.1	
14	170 S.W. 1.5 S.	39.5	8	17	118.5	24.5	57.2	12.4 .8 (4) 1.4 1.4 .8 .5 1.0						.1 (4) .1 .0 .1 .0 .1	320	65.3	131.9	.8	"	76,000	60,800	92.4	
15	150 S.W. 1.5 N.	39.0	8	17	125.5		64.4	5.6 (4) 2.2 .9 .9 .7 .8						.3 (2) .3 .3 .3 .3 .2	92	49.6	119.6	4.0	"	34,200	27,400	80.6	
16	152 S.W. 1.5 S.	39.0	8	17	118.5		63.0	5.6 (4) 2.8 2.2 1.4 1.6 1.3						.2 (4) .2 .1 .2 .1 .1	91	42.9	111.5	2.0	"	30,400	24,300	82.5	
17	130 S.W. 1.5 N.	35.0	8	17	127.5		62.3	.2 .10 (8) 8.6 (4) 1.6 1.0 .8 .6						.2 .5 .2 .1 .1 .1	63	35.8	98.3	2.4	"	26,800	21,400	63.6	
18	130 S.W. 1.5 S.	35.0	8	17	127.5		64.2	9.7 (4) 1.5 1.2 .9 1.1 .8						.2 (3) .2 .2 .2 .1 .1	103	44.5	120.4	2.4	"	40,200	32,200	95.4	
19	108 S.W. 1.5 N.	48.5	8	17	104.5		67.0	2.6 (3) 1.6 2.0 1.8 .7 1.3						.8 (2) .4 .2 .4 .5 .3	27	27.0	96.6	5.2	"	14,700	11,800	48.1	Piles could not be driven
20	106 S.W. 1.5	48.5	8	17	104.5		66.7	3.1 2.8 (3) 3.0 2.0 2.2 1.6 1.4						.7 (3) .8 .3 .4 .5 .4	25	26.3	96.1	6.2	"	12,100	10,200	48.2	further, for lack of equipment
21	88 S.W. 1.5 N.	50.0	8	17	105.0		70.6	3.2 2.8 (3) 3.0 1.2 2.0 1.8 6.6						.1 (4) .2 .2 .2 .3 .2	26	27.2	101.0	2.0	"	45,600	36,500	51.0	
22	88 S.W. 1.5 S.	50.0	8	17	104.5		68.3	7.2 2.0 (3) 2.0 1.8 1.4 1.4 1.4						.1 (4) .2 .1 .2 .1 .1	24	19.6	95.1	1.2	"	41,500	33,200	45.1	
23	650 S.W. 1.5 N.	53.0	8	17	107.0		73.1	6.8 2.0 (3) 2.6 1.1 .6 .4 .2						.2 (3) .2 .1 .1 .1 .1	16	8.7	88.6	1.8	"	40,000	34.6	Tip broomed 10' Rock at -
24	675 S.W. 1.5 S.	53.0	8	17	106.5		73.9	3.4 2.5 (3) 3.1 .4 .2 .2						.1 (3) .1 .1 .1 .1 .1	14	7.2	86.0	1.4	"	40,000	31.0	" " 10 "
25	500 S.W. 1.5 N.	54.0	8	17	108.0		72.3	.1 (4) .11 .1 .2 .1						.1 (5) .1 .1 .1 .1 .1	10	2.6	75.5	1.2	"	40,000	"	.5' Rock - 7
26	490 S.W. 1.5 S.	54.0	8	17	107.5		72.6	.3 .5 (4) .1 .1 .1						.1 (8) .2 .1 .0 .1 .0	9	2.1	73.9	1.0	"	"	19.4	" .5' Rock - 7
27	380 S.W. 1.5 N.	54.5	8	17	82.0		68.7	.6 .6 (4) 1.6 1.3 .4 .2 .1						.1 (6) 0 (8) .2 .0 .2 .0	12	3.6	72.9	.6	"	"		18.4	Pile on Rock
28	380 S.W. 1.5 S.	54.5	8	17	82.0		63.5	7.7 .7 (4) .6 .2 .4 (4) .1 .2						.2 (4) .1 .0 .1 .0 .2	13	2.7	73.9	1.2	"	"		18.9	Tip broomed 5' Rock -
29	200 S.W. 1.5 N.	54.5	8	17	82.0		61.5	.1 .3 (4) 0 (4) .1 .1 .2 .1 (4)						.1 (5) .0 .1 .0 .0 .0	15	2.4	64.0	1.2	"	"		9.5	Pile on Rock
30	200 S.W. 1.5 S.	54.5	8	17	82.0		61.4	1.3 .6 (4) .4 .1 .1 .2						.1 (8) .2 .6 .2 .2 .2	14	2.6	65.3	1.4	"	"		10.8	
31	10 W. 1.5 N.	43.3	5	16	83.3		43.5	7.0 .8 (4) 1.6 1.0 .4 .5						.1 (8) .2 .2 .2 .2 .1	62	23.3	73.8	.6	"	"		22.5	Tip broomed 2 slight 8" Rock
32	10 W. 1.5 S.	43.3	5	16	75.1		7.7	6.8 (4) 2.0 .2 .2 .1 .1 .1						.1 (4) .1 .1 .1 .1 .2	14	2.3	66.2	1.2	"	"		22.0	Tip broomed 10" Rock
33	180 E. 1.5 N.	27.0	8	14	68.0	24.5	42.7	13.0 .1 (3) 1.7 1.7 1.9 2.8 1.4						.1 (3) 0 .0 .1 .0 .0	51	14.6	70.3	.6	"	"		39.8	Tip broomed 3.5' Rock
34	180 E. 1.5 S.	26.6	9	14	64.5	24.5	42.2	7.9 .2 (3) 3.0 2.7 2.4 2.3 .2						.1 (4) .0 .0 .1 .0 .0	18	15.0	65.1	.6	"	"		38.0	Tip broomed .5' Rock
35	380 E. 1.5 N.	20.2	8	14	70.6	24.5	33.9	7.4 3.8 (3) 3.2 2.7 2.8 1.6 .5						.1 (2) .0 .0 .1 .0 .0	36	27.4	68.7	.4	"	"		48.5	Tip slightly broomed
36	380 E. 1.5 S.	22.5	8	14	70.6	24.5	36.0	9.3 .3 (3) 3.2 2.6 2.5 2.0 .6						.1 (2) .0 .1 .0 .0 .0	43	26.0	71.3	.4	"	"		46.2	Tip broomed 2.6' Rock
37	590 E. 1.5 N.	22.0	7	14	82.5	24.5	41.1	11.0 (8) .3 .2 1.1 2.7 2.8 1.6						.1 (2) .1 .0 .1 .0 .0	114	31.8	83.9	.4	"	"		50.4	Pile broke 11.5 from tip Rock
38	570 E. 1.5 S.	23.0	8	14	71.0	24.5	38.2	9.6 3.2 (3) 3.0 2.6 2.6 1.4 .9						.1 (3) .0 .1 .0 .0 .0	38	25.5	73.3	.6	"	"		50.3	Tip slightly broomed
39	780 E. 1.5 N.	19.5	8	17	83.0		25.7	3.7 .3 (8) 4.8 6.0 3.5 3.4 2.7						.1 (4) .1 .1 .1 .1 .1	45	41.7	61.2	1.2	"	41,500	33,200	56.6	
40	780 E. 1.5 S.	20.2	8	17	83.0	24.5	40.7	6.2 (4) 2.5 3.8 2.2 1.9 1.0						.1 (4) .1 .1 .1 .1 .0	54	31.9	79.5	.8	"	50,600	40,500	60.0	
41	980 E. 1.5 N.	15.7	8	17	83.0		28.3	7.6 (6) 6.6 3.9 1.2 1.4 1.0						.0 (4) .1 .1 .1 .1 .1	65	33.0	68.9	1.0	"	45,600	36,500	53.2	
42	980 E. 1.5 S.	14.5	7	16.5	75.0		33.3	6.1 .2 (4) 2.7 1.7 1.3 1.8 1.6						.1 .3 .2 .2 .2 .3	67	29.8	67.2	2.6	"	25,300	20,200	52.7	

Revised 2-14-16

Distances from Savannah Pier Head are from Stadia readings
Piles over 85' long were spliced at butt end by means of 4 timbers
6"x 8"x 21' long and 12-1" dia bolts.

Specifications for Driving Test Piles in the North River Approximately on a Line Running from Canal Street, Manhattan, to Twelfth Street, Jersey City.

Test piles are to be driven in the bottom of the North River between bulkhead lines of New York City and Jersey City on a line between Canal Street, New York City, and Twelfth Street, Jersey City, or adjacent thereto as directed by the Engineer in charge.

These piles will be driven in water varying in depth up to perhaps 60 ft. as a maximum. The piles will be driven to varying depths as may be directed by the Engineer in charge, but the contractor must provide piles and apparatus capable of driving and pulling piles 130 ft. in length below the surface of the water.

It will be advisable to employ a scow or barge fitted with pile driving leads suitable for driving long piles at any point on the line indicated, as it will be necessary to drive a considerable number of test piles to be pulled after being driven to refusal or to such other less depth as may be directed.

The number of these test piles cannot be determined in advance but there may be as many as 50 or more. Some of these test piles may be employed to ascertain the depth of rock. On account of the great depth of water in the river it will be necessary to provide for the splicing of piles at some points, at least, for these test purposes. Such splicing must be made with the greatest effectiveness possible and in a manner approved by the Engineer in charge of the work.

A complete record must be made of all the circumstances or conditions developed in the driving of these test piles, including the depth penetrated at each blow of the hammer, the total number of blows corresponding to the depth, the depth first penetrated by own weight of the pile or pile and hammer, the resistance encountered in withdrawing the pile and all other features or circumstances disclosed which may bear upon the carrying capacity of the material penetrated.

Contractors will name prices on making not less than 30 tests, basing their prices on the following schedule. For tests including driving and pulling of piles if the required total penetration in water and mud below M. L. W. level is—

        not in excess of 70 ft.—price per lineal ft.
        from 70 to 90 ft.—price per lineal foot.
        " 90 " 110 "— " " " "
        " 110 " 130 "— " " " "

Above prices must include all charges for plant, labor, delay, loss and damage.

RESULTS OF BORINGS

No.	Location	Sand	Clay and Silt	Gravel	Rock
	NEW JERSEY				
1	Southeast corner 13th and Grove Streets	—10 to—50.0'		0 to— 10.0'	—50.' to— 54.0'
2	175.0' west of west P. L. of Henderson St., 90.0' south of south P. L. of 13th Street	0 to—64.0'			—64.0' to— 94.0'
3	Northwest corner 12th & Henderson Streets	0 to—50.0'			—50.0' to— 65.0'
4	125.0' east of east P. L. of Henderson St., south side 12th Street	0 to—60.0'			—60.0' to— 75.0'
5	30.0' west of west P. L. of Provost St. on south walk of 12th Street	0 to—50.0'			—50.0' to— 80.0'
6	103.0' east of east P. L. of Provost St., 9.33' south of north P. L. of 12th Street	0 to—59.0'			—59.0' to— 89.0'
7	303.0' east of east P. L. of Provost St., 7.0' north of south P. L. of 12th St.	0 to—71.75'			—71.75' to— 86.0'
8	Southwest corner D., L. & W. property and southeast corner of lumber yard	—30.0' to—68.75'	0 to— 30.0'		—68.75' to— 86.0'
9	75.0' west of south pole on D., L. & W. property and 45.0' east of north pole	0 to—71.0'			—71.0' to— 82.0'
10	30.0' west of west end of fence and 33.0' east of northwest corner of tool house on D., L. & W. property	—30.0 to—72.0'	0 to— 30.0'		—72.0' to— 83.83'
11	200.0' west of Hole #14 on C. L. 12th St. produced	0 to—20.0' —30.0 to—75.0'	—20.0' to— 30.0'		—75.0' to— 80.0'
12	200.0' west of Hole #13 on C. L. 12th St. produced	0 to—20.0' —40.0' to—68.0'	—20.0 to— 40.0'		—68.0' to— 76.0'
13	200.0' west of Hole #12 on C. L. 12th St. produced	0 to—20.0' —50.0' to—80.33'	—20.0' to— 50.0'		—80.33' to— 90.0'
14	C. L. 12th Street produced and Hudson River	—70.0' to—98.0'	0 to— 70.0'		—98.0' to—113.0'
	NEW YORK				
17	Intersection C. L. Canal and West Streets	—24.0' to—98.17'	0 to— 24.0'		— 98.17' to—128.17'
18	North side Canal between Washington and West Streets	0 to—92.0'			—92.0' to—100.0'

RESULTS OF BORINGS

Hole No.	Location	Sand	Clay and Silt	Gravel	Rock
	NEW YORK				
29	South side Canal between Washington and West Streets	0 to —91.0'			—91.0' to— 98.0'
30	Northwest corner Washington and Canal Sts.	0 to—92.0'			—92.0' to— 98.0'
31	Northwest corner Greenwich and Canal Streets	0 to—82.83'			—82.83' to— 89.0'
32	Southwest corner Greenwich and Canal Streets	0 to—96.25'			— 96.25' to—111.25'
33	Southeast corner Greenwich and Canal Streets	0 to—90.0'			—90.0' to—100.0'
34	East corner Renwick and Canal Streets	0 to—122.0'			—122.0' to—144.5'
35	Southwest corner Watts and Canal Streets	0 to—99.0'			—99.0' to—114.0'
36	Southeast corner Hudson and Canal Streets	0 to—84.0'			—84.0' to— 99.0'
37	North side Canal between Hudson and Varick Sts.	0 to—10.0' —21.5' to—84.33'		—10.0' to— 21.5'	—84.33' to—100.0'
38	Southeast corner Canal and Varick Streets	0 to—50.0'			—50.0' to— 61.5'

Hole No.	Location	Water	Sand	Clay and Silt	Gravel	Rock
	RIVER					
	All river borings taken on a C. L. between the south corner of Savannah Line pier and the north corner of Erie Pier #9.					
15	350.0' west of bulkhead Erie #9	—9.90'	—104.90' to—134.90'	— 9.90' to—104.90'	—134.90' to—139.83'	—139.83' to—145.83'
16	123.0' west of Erie Pierhead #9	—6.60'		— 6.60' to—162.80'		—162.80' to—169.80'
17	300.0' east of Erie #9	—24.30'		—24.30' to—244.93'		—244.93' to—249.88'
18	700.0' " " " #9	—33.50'		—33.50' to—259.35'		—259.35' to—266.12'
19	1,100.0' " " " #9	—32.0'		—32.0' to—253.35'		—253.35' to—256.15'
20	2,100.0' west of Savannah Line Pier	—33.0'		—33.0' to—248.5'		—248.5' to—264.23'
21	1,850.0' west of Savannah Line Pier	—35.4'	—197.0' to—203.7'	—35.0' to—197.0'		—203.7' to—207.5'
22	1,450.0' west of Savannah Line Pier	—38.0'	—165.5' to—168.3'	—38.0' to—165.5'		—168.3' to—171.7'
23	1,050.0' west of Savannah Line Pier	—43.0'	—122.4' to—125.4'	—43.0' to—122.4'		—125.4' to—135.35'
24	650.0' west of Savannah Line Pier	—52.0'		—52.0' to— 83.6'		—83.6' to—132.15'
25	250.0' west of Savannah Line Pier	—54.5'		—54.5' to— 64.0'		—64.0' to— 78.1'
26	400.0' east of Savannah Line Pierhead	—20.20'		—20.20' to— 70.33'		—70.33' to— 79.33'

Note—About 1.0' of sand and gravel was found on rock.

APPENDIX No. 3.

STUDIES FOR THE PILE FOUNDATION OF THE RIVER SECTION OF THE TUNNEL.

It is imperative in the method of tunnel construction contemplated in the report that the foundation piles driven in the bottom of the dredged trench be placed and cut off with the highest degree of accuracy attainable. It is the purpose of these studies to outline effective methods of accomplishing those ends within the shortest practicable time as the tidal currents may tend to refill the trench. The plans shown on Plates Nos. 9 and 10 have been developed only far enough to show the practicability of the methods which they indicate. The procedure is substantially the use of a framed template for either a single transverse bent of piles or for a considerable number of bents, so that by one placing of the template a number of piles may be accurately driven and cut off before moving it. It will be observed that the method of supporting the template, as well as the pile drivers or saws resting on it, is such as to make the operations independent of the tide. The driving of the piles through the cylinders of the templates permits the use of any effective steel follower or any other special devices that may be found practicable.

The large steel frame template shown on Plate No. 9 may be partially floated to any extent desired by the steel air cylinders shown, so as to reduce the weight resting upon the last bent of piles cut off and on the spuds holding the advancing end of it in position while the piles are being driven and cut off.

APPENDIX No. 4.

STUDIES FOR SPECIAL FORMS OF TUBES AND METHODS OF PLACING THEM NEAR BULKHEADS.

The plans shown on Plates Nos. 11 and 12 are developments of the pneumatic and open dredging methods adapted to the conditions found on the New York side from the outer limit of the rock excavation to the bulkhead and between the pierhead and bulkhead on the New Jersey side. As stated in the report the estimate of cost made by the Board is based upon the special forms of tube adapted to the pneumatic method, although the work could also be done by the open dredging method.

The plans have been developed only so far as is necessary to assure effective treatment for the parts of the work indicated and sufficient for the purposes of making a reliable estimate of cost. Like other plans of these appendices they are not intended for working plans.

APPENDIX No. 5.

DETAILS OF ESTIMATE OF COST.

The following sheets show in full detail the estimate of cost for the various parts of the work, including the ventilating shafts on either side of the river and one intermediate shaft for the New Jersey approach, the ventilating plant, the electric power installation for driving the ventilating plant, the electric lighting installation and the telephones.

The data shown on the sheets are self explanatory except as to the general specifications on which the prices are based.

These general specifications may be stated as those of the Committees of the American Society of Civil Engineers and of the American Society for Testing Materials for cement and concrete, and the American Railway Engineering Association Specifications for such steel work as has been covered by the estimate of cost. It has been the intention of the Board that the entire work should be at least equal in quality or excellence to similar classes of work done under the Specifications of the Board of Water Supply and the Public Service Commission of New York City. Complete specifications adapted to the work contemplated must be fully developed on which to base actual working plans and the operations of construction.

ESTIMATE OF COST

Walls and pavement at tunnel entrance (460' in N. Y., 450' in N. J.)

12,000 cu. yds. excavation @	$0.88 cu. yd.	$10,560.
1,685 " " conc. in floors @	4.00 " "	6,740.
1,940 " " " " walls @	4.50 " "	8,730.
2,400 sq. yds. pavement @	2.00 sq. yd.	4,800.
2 ticket houses, each @	1,350.	2,700.
327 sq. yds. street pavement @	2.50 sq. yd.	817.50
	Total	$34,347.50

Note: Cost per linear foot—$37.75

Approach Section (1,400 ft. in New Jersey and 340 ft. in New York.)

15,660 cu. yds. concrete @	$7.50 cu. yd.	$117,450.
2,175 tons of reinforcing steel @	0.04 per lb.	174,000.
3,480 sq. yds. pavement @	2.00 sq. yd.	6,960.
27,610 cu. yds. dry excavation @	0.67 cu. yd.	18,498.70
30,940 " " wet " @	1.10 " "	34,034.
99,400 sq. ft. of sheeting @	0.67 sq. ft.	66,598.
200,000 ft. B. M. of bracing to be used twice		
Material 200,000' B. M. @	44.50 per M.	8,900.
Labor 400,000' B. M. @	27.00 " "	10,800.
40,000 cu. yds. excav. to dispose of @	0.20 cu. yd.	8,000.
135,000 ft. B. M. decking @	70.00 per M.	9,450.
5,973 sq. yds. street pavement @	2.50 sq. yd.	14,932.50
Pumping		10,000.
	Total	$479,623.20

Note: Cost per linear foot—$275.65

Shafts

3,600 cu. yds. concrete	@	$8.00 cu. yd.	$28,800.
160,000 cubical displacement of building	@	0.50 cu. ft.	80,000.
40 tons of reinforcing steel	@	0.40 per lb.	3,200.
Shaft on N. J. approach			30,000.
		Total	$142,000.

From Approach Section to Shafts

985 ft. in N. Y.
980 ft. in N. J.

25,300 cu. yds. concrete	@	$8.50 cu. yd.	$215,050.
1,570 tons of reinforcing steel	@	0.04 lb.	125,600.
3,710 sq. yds. pavement	@	2.00 sq. yd.	7,420.
38,800 cu. yds. dry excavation			
19,350	@	0.67 cu. yd.	12,964.50
19,440	@	1.35 " "	26,244.
103,800 cu. yds. wet excavation			
50,600	@	1.20 " "	60,720.
53,200	@	1.90 " "	101,080.
63,900 cu. yds. excav to dispose of	@	0.20 " "	12,780.
51,100 sq. ft. sheeting above water	@	0.67 sq. ft.	34,237.
173,000 sq. ft. sheeting below water	@	1.35 " "	233,550.
862,500 ft. B. M. bracing	@	43.00 per M.	37,087.50
1,150,000 ft. B. M. "	@	27.00 " "	31,050.
900,000 ft. B. M. decking	@	71.50 " "	64,350.
2,500 ft. of 8' sewer to remove, maintain and replace			187,500.
1,000 ft. of 3' x 4' oval brick sewer	@	15.00 per ft.	15,000.
100 ft. of 4' brick sewer	@	15.00 per ft.	1,500.
Property Damage, N. Y. side			
2,040'	@	25.00 " "	51,000.
Property Damage, N. J. Side			
1,500'	@	25.00 " "	37,500.
100'	@	100.00 " "	10,000.
7,000 sq. yds. street pavement	@	2.50 sq. yd.	17,500.
		Total	$1,282,133.00

Note: Cost per linear foot—$652.48

No Piles Required

TUNNEL SECTIONS UNDER AIR

1,900 ft. in N. Y.
1,100 ft. in N. J.

209,200 cu. yds. excavation	@	$2.00 cu. yd.	$418,400.
115,000 " " " to dispose of	@	0.20 " "	23,000.
16,400 lin ft. of piles	@	3.00 lin. ft.	49,200.
Rock excavation			100,000.
54,200 cu. yds. concrete	@	7.50 cu. yd.	406,500.
15,000 " " " (under air)	@	10.00 " "	150,000.
9,000 " " " (seal, under air)	@	8.00 " "	72,000.
2,400 tons of reinforcing steel	@	0.04 per lb.	192,000.
2,850 " " " " (under air)	@	0.0475 " "	270,750.

33 tunnel sections and joints, complete	@	6,000.	198,000.
Timber crib above working chamber, 4,200,000' B. M.	@	65.00 per M.	273,000.
Bracing in working chamber, 550,000' B. M.	@	70.00 " "	38,500.
255 tons of steel in cutting edge	@	0.054 " lb.	27,540.
5,670 sq. yds. pavement	@	2.00 sq. yd.	11,340.
		Total	$2,230,230.

Note: Cost per linear foot—$743.41

RIVER SECTION

2,680 ft. of tunnel

810,000 cu. yds. dredging	@	$0.70 cu. yd.	$567,000.
42,900 " " concrete	@	7.50 " "	321,750.
4,820 tons of steel reinforcement	@	0.04 per lb.	385,600.
5,067 sq. yds. pavement	@	2.00 sq. yd.	10,134.
33 tunnel sections and joints, complete	@	$5,000.	165,000.
2,010 piles, each	@	67.50	135,675.
Cost of removing cables			8,000.
		Total	$1,593,159.

Note: Cost per linear foot—$594.46

Drainage

Cost of 6 centrifugal pumps and 20,000 ft. of 8" c. i. drain pipe in place	$40,000.
Maintenance and replacement of existing water lines " " " " " gas " " " " " " electric conduits " " " " " sewers (N. Y. side only)	$250,000.

D. L. & W. Yard

2,600 lin. ft. of yard track to take up and replace, also trainmen's shed to remove and replace *Provost Street* One story corr. iron 60' x 80' store house to remove and replace	$2,500
One story frame shed 60' x 44' to remove and replace, also 2,000 ft. of E. R. R. track in 12th Street to take up and replace	$2,500.
Total	$ 295,000.

Waterproofing	716,000 sq. ft. @ $0.05	35,800.
	308,000 sq. ft. @ 0.10	30,800.
	744,000 sq. ft. @ 0.25	186,000.
Ventilating Plant, present cost		120,000.
" " power installation, present cost		20,000.
Electric light installation, present cost		34,000.
" " emergency system, present cost		15,000.
Telephones		1,000.
Engineering, 5%		300,000.
Extra work not provided for		100,000.
	Grand Total	$6,899,092.70

APPENDIX No. 6.

STUDIES FOR TUBE JOINTS.

There are a number of safe and effective methods of joining sections of such tunnel tubes as those contemplated in this report. Similar devices have been used in works like the Detroit River Tunnel and the latest subway tunnel under the Harlem River. The joint must be made in this case under a head of water varying from 50 ft. to 80 ft. and it must be of such a character as to maintain the continuity of the tube with practically its full transverse resistance. Methods shown on Plate No. 8A may be developed in the working drawings so as to produce these results. As they stand they are only developed to indicate the feasibility and practicability of completing a joint in place possessing the characteristics of continuity and strength desired. Other methods may be developed to accomplish the same purpose.

APPENDIX No. 7.

TENTATIVE CONSIDERATIONS REGARDING THE VEHICLE TRAFFIC OF SOME OF THE FERRIES CROSSING THE HUDSON RIVER AND THEIR BEARING UPON THE USE OF THE PROPOSED TUNNEL AND ITS VENTILATION.

Investigations made by Mr. Percy Ingalls have determined that no continuous records of vehicular traffic between Manhattan and New Jersey are available. From a two day actual count made in 1913 it would appear that the total daily east and westbound vehicular traffic over five ferries adjacent to the location of the proposed tunnel amounted to 9,718 vehicles or slightly over one-half of the daily total for all ferries between New York and New Jersey. In 1916 a ten hour count on two consecutive days for the same ferries indicated an increase of 11.91% over the corresponding hours in 1913 or at the rate of nearly 4% increase in traffic per year. Certain incomplete reports from the companies operating the ferries indicate a lower percentage of increase in the traffic. Assuming that the normal 1916 traffic amounts to 11,000 vehicles per week day and a future increase of only 2½% per year, then the normal week day traffic to be anticipated for the district corresponding to the five ferries will be:

		Yearly Total
In 1920 over 12,140	(For a year of 350	4,249,000
" 1925 " 13,740	average days)	4,809,000
" 1930 " 15,540		5,439,000

In recent years an increasing proportion of this traffic is motor driven, the percentage being 10% in 1913; 19½% in 1915; and 23.3% in 1916, or an increase of 13.3% in three years. If this rate of increase in the future is reduced to 3% per year, the percentage of motor driven vehicles to total vehicles to be anticipated for the downtown district will be nearly 35% in 1920, 50% in 1925, and 65% in 1930 and the motor traffic for the downtown district would be

    In 1920................................ 4,249 motors
    " 1925................................ 6,870 "
    " 1930................................10,101 "

This Board anticipates some such steady increase in the number of motor driven vehicles, and, in order to make provision for the maximum probable use of the tunnel, has considered that on days when navigation on the river is impeded by fog, ice, or other adverse conditions all of the motor vehicles in the district now served by the five downtown ferries would seek the tunnel, and that, therefore, ventilation and other facilities should be provided for not less than 10,000 motors with the possibility of increasing facilities so as to provide against double this number.

On test days the maximum hourly traffic for east and west traffic was 7¾% and the maximum hourly one way traffic was 4.6% of the total for the day. A daily use of the tunnel by 20,000 vehicles would on this basis bring in the peak hour, 920 vehicles per hour for one roadway and 1,550 on two roadways. Their use would be met by maintaining an average center to center interval of 60 ft. with a speed of about 10 miles per hour.

The maximum capacity of the tunnel will be attained by a continuous movement of vehicles at a high uniform speed and with the minimum safe interval between vehicles. The speed of motor trucks is automatically regulated and a rate of ten to twelve miles per hour may be taken as the practical rate for heavy motor trucks. At that speed this Board considers that the center to center distance for safety should not be less than 60 ft. At ten miles per hour and with 60 ft. intervals the capacity of a single roadway is 880 vehicles per hour. The number of vehicles in the section between the shafts would be at the time of maximum two way use $\dfrac{5{,}550 \times 2}{60} = 183$ vehicles. From the foregoing, it appears that the probable maximum use of the tunnel may equal the capacity. The capacity would be reduced if slow moving horse drawn trucks were allowed to interfere with fast moving motors.

The Board has assumed as a basis for the calculation of the ventilation required that there may be for the entire length of the tunnel and for a considerable period of time two lines of motors moving in opposite directions spaced uniformly 60 ft. center to center, and also that as a result of a block there might be the same number of motors congested in a 4,000 ft. length of tunnel.

APPENDIX No. 8.

LIGHTING OF PROPOSED VEHICULAR TUNNEL.

There will be 1,000 lighting fixtures, comprised of 500 on each side of the tunnel, each spaced approximately 20 ft. apart. The contemplated scheme for illumination will be a system of indirect lighting; that is, the projection of the light rays on the ceiling and reflection therefrom uniformly distributed throughout the tunnel without the glare of the light source being visible.

Each outlet for each lighting fixture will be equipped with a 100 Watt type "C" lamp. The fixtures will be of the high efficiency projecting type.

In addition to this general lighting system which will be supplied with current from the commercial lighting service, there has been planned a separate and distinct lighting service of the same type, but to be comprised of only 200 fixtures, 100 on each side of the tunnel, each spaced 100 ft. apart. This system is to be used in emergency in case the commercial lighting service should fail temporarily and will be supplied with current from a 200 ampere hour storage battery equipped with automatic control, which will furnish capacity sufficient to light 200 fixtures for a period of one hour, thus assuring, in case of a breakdown of the commercial service, a diminished illumination sufficient to permit the safe operation of vehicles in the tunnel.

The general lighting system and emergency lighting system will be interconnected by time limit and non-voltage relays, automatically opening and closing the various switches in event of a breakdown in the commercial lighting service.

The estimated cost of the initial installation for the general lighting is $37,750.00, based on present day prices, and the cost of the initial installation for the emergency lighting will be $16,670.00, based on present day prices. Estimates are attached herewith.

The lighting load will, of course, be continuous and will require 100 KW constantly. This amounts to 73,000 KW hours per month, which will cost $991.58 per month or $11,899.00 per year, based on wholesale rate of 1.63c per KW, which rate will apply for the current consumption of the lighting load as the lighting load will be taken from the same commercial service and transformer supplying the current for power purposes.

GENERAL LIGHTING

1000	Outlets	$ 600.00
37000'	#10 Duplex rubber and lead 2400. V.	8,500.00
25000'	#10 " " " braid 600. V.	1,000.00
20	5 KW transformers	2,000.00
20	Primary cutouts	500.00
25000'	¾" conduit	2,700.00
37000'	1" "	5,500.00
1000	100 W. type "C" lamps	650.00
1000	Lighting fixtures	10,000.00
20	Secondary fused cutouts	300.00
	Switchboards, controls, relays	5,000.00
	Contingencies	1,000.00
		$37,750.00

EMERGENCY LIGHTING

200	Outlets	$ 120.00
46000'	#8 single R. C. & Br.	2,200.00
6000'	#6 " " "	450.00
6000'	#4 " " "	600.00
6000'	#3 " " "	690.00
12000'	#2 " " "	1,680.00
6000'	#1 " " "	1,100.00
22000'	1" conduit	2,420.00
6000	1¼" "	1,180.00
4000	1½" "	880.00
20	Fused cutouts	300.00
1	200 ampere storage battery	3,000.00
1	50 KW charging set	1,050.00
1	Main battery switchboard	1,000.00
		$16,670.00

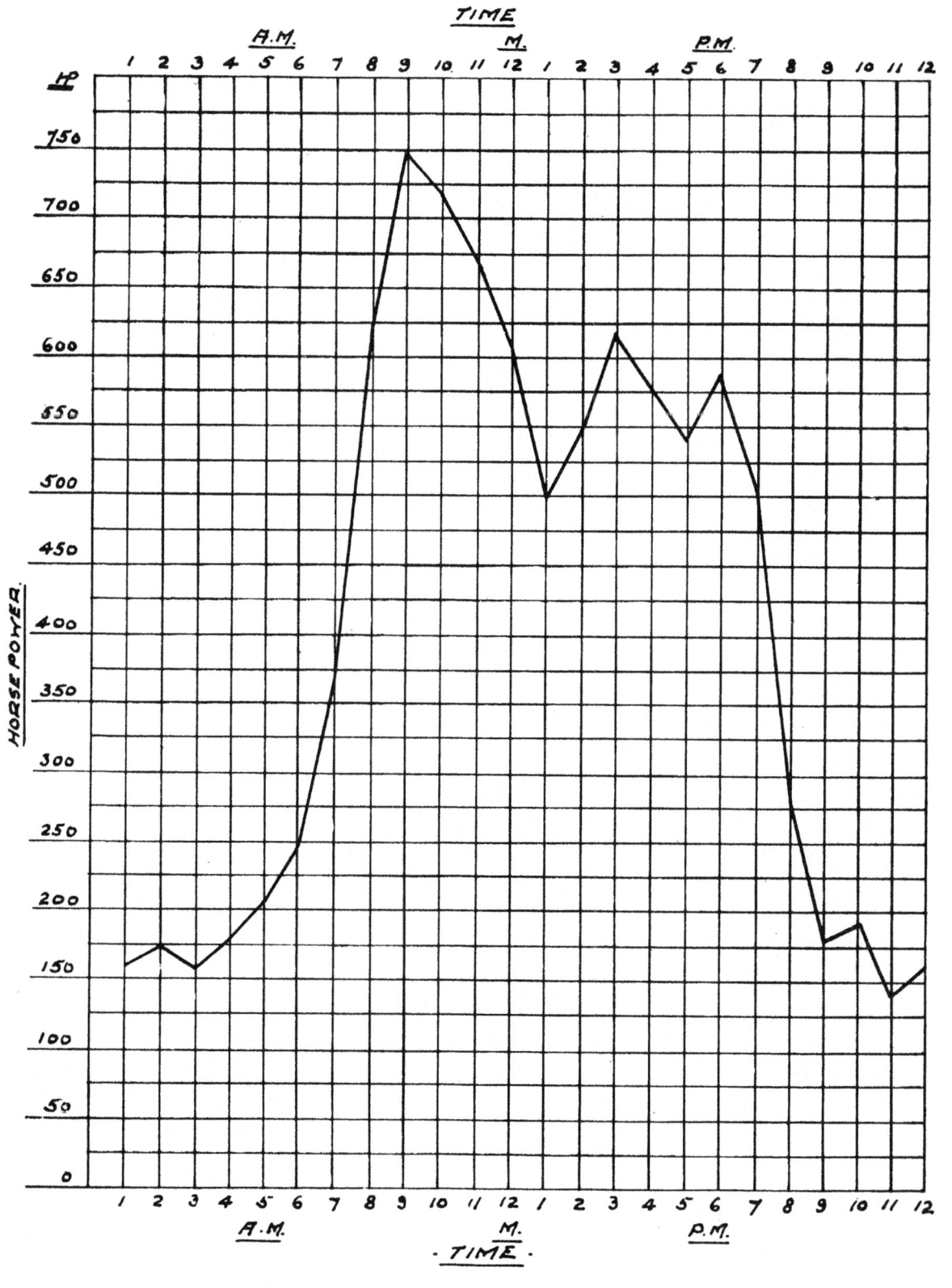

APPENDIX No. 9.

FORCE REQUIRED TO OPERATE THE TUNNEL.

The statement given below shows an effective organization for the operation of the entire tunnel, including the ventilating and lighting plants. The force indicated is sufficient for traffic likely to be developed for a considerable period of years after the opening of the tunnel.

	Per Shift	Total	Rate	Daily Amount
Superintendence				
Superintendent	($2,500 per year)	1	$7.00	$ 7.00 (nearly)
Asst. Superintendent	($1,800 " ")	1	5.00	5.00 "
Clerk	($1,500 " ")	1	4.00	4.00 "
Operation of Machinery				
Operators	2	6	$3.00	$18.00
Helpers	3	9	2.50	22.50
Electrician	1	3	3.50	10.50
Police				
2 in tunnel—2 at entrance	4	12	$3.00	$36.00
Ticket Takers, Sweepers, Etc.				
Ticket Takers	2	6	$3.00	$18.00
Sweepers and Cleaners		8	2.25	18.00
Total				$139.00

Per year @ 300 days for sweepers .... $ 5,400.
  "   "   " 365 "   " others .... 44,125.

Total .... $49,525.

APPENDIX No. 10.

INVESTIGATIONS REGARDING THE VITIATION OF THE AIR IN THE TESTING HOUSE AT PASSAIC WHARF BY ACTUAL OPERATION OF GASOLINE MOTOR VEHICLES, INCLUDING CHEMICAL ANALYSIS.

GELLERT ALLEMAN
SWARTHMORE
PENNSYLVANIA

February 16, 1917.

Analyses of Air in Experimental Tunnel.

Mr. Martin Schreiber,
Engineer Maintenance of Way,
Public Service Corporation,
Newark, N. J.

Dear Sir:—

I herewith enclose the results obtained on analyzing samples of air taken from experimental tunnel.

The conditions under which these samples were taken are indicated in the report, and only the actual figures obtained, together with the conclusions drawn, are presented. The accompanying blue print indicates, at a glance, the average results obtained on analyzing the air taken from the experimental tunnel.

Should you desire details regarding the collection of samples, the methods employed for analyzing these gases, and the special apparatus which was necessary to have constructed in order to collect and analyze these gases, I shall be glad to send you such information.

Very truly yours,

GELLERT ALLEMAN.

RESULTS OF

AIR ANALYSES

IN

EXPERIMENTAL TUNNEL

Test #1: Date 1/22/17

Conditions:

All doors and ventilators closed. Engines of eight cars (arranged as in diagram) all racing for thirty minutes.

WEST END

	1	2	3	Average
Unsaturated Hydro carbons....	0.28%	0.28%	0.39%	0.32%
Carbon dioxide	0.58%	0.60%	0.62%	0.60%
Oxygen	19.10%	19.07%	18.99%	19.05%
Carbon monoxide	0.61%	0.64%	0.39%	0.55%

	4	5	6	
Unsaturated Hydro carbons....	—	—	0.18%	0.18%
Carbon dioxide	—	—	1.15%	1.15%
Oxygen	—	—	17.45%	17.45%
Carbon monoxide	—	—	0.51%	0.51%

	7	8	9	
Unsaturated Hydro carbons....	0.22%	0.67%	0.31%	0.38%
Carbon dioxide	0.54%	0.56%	0.21%	0.44%
Oxygen	19.03%	19.50%	18.67%	19.07%
Carbon monoxide	0.61%	0.64%	0.45%	0.57%

Averages

Unsaturated Hydro carbons....	0.25%	0.48%	0.29%
Carbon dioxide	0.56%	0.58%	0.66%
Oxygen	19.06%	19.28%	18.37%
Carbon monoxide	0.61%	0.64%	0.45%

Average for West End

Unsaturated Hydro carbons	0.34%
Carbon dioxide	0.60%
Oxygen	18.90%
Carbon monoxide	0.57%

EAST END

	10	11	12	Average
Unsaturated Hydro carbons....	—	0.40%	0.06%	0.23%
Carbon dioxide	—	0.41%	0.50%	0.45%
Oxygen	—	19.08%	19.42%	19.25%
Carbon monoxide	—	0.63%	0.44%	0.54%

	13	14	15	
Unsaturated Hydro carbons....	0.13%	0.45%	0.02%	0.20%
Carbon dioxide	0.43%	0.39%	0.41%	0.41%
Oxygen	19.14%	19.07%	19.23%	19.15%
Carbon monoxide	0.41%	0.93%	0.51%	0.62%

	16	17	18	
Unsaturated Hydro carbons	—	0.03%	—	0.03%
Carbon dioxide	—	0.33%	—	0.33%
Oxygen	—	19.39%	—	19.39%
Carbon monoxide	—	1.12%	—	1.12%

Averages

Unsaturated Hydro carbons	0.13%	0.29%	0.04%
Carbon dioxide	0.43%	0.38%	0.46%
Oxygen	19.14%	19.18%	19.33%
Carbon monoxide	0.41%	0.89%	0.48%

Average for East End

Unsaturated Hydro carbons	0.51%
Carbon dioxide	0.42%
Oxygen	19.22%
Carbon monoxide	0.59%

Test #2: Date 1/24/17

Conditions:

All doors and ventilators closed. Engines of eight cars (arranged as in diagram) all running light for thirty minutes.

WEST END

	1	2	3	Average
Unsaturated Hydro carbons	*0.01%	*0.01%	0.02%	0.01%
Carbon dioxide	0.09%	0.18%	0.16%	0.14%
Oxygen	18.81%	20.12%	20.10%	19.68%
Carbon monoxide	0.32%	0.56%	0.36%	0.41%

	4	5	6	
Unsaturated Hydro carbons	0.01%	*0.01%	*0.01%	*0.01%
Carbon dioxide	0.09%	0.08%	0.11%	0.09%
Oxygen	19.40%	20.09%	20.14%	19.88%
Carbon monoxide	0.41%	0.41%	0.62%	0.48%

*Less.

	7	8	9	
Unsaturated Hydro carbons	0.01%	0.02%	0.02%	0.02%
Carbon dioxide	0.15%	0.07%	0.09%	0.10%
Oxygen	18.74%	18.63%	20.89%	19.42%
Carbon monoxide	0.62%	0.56%	0.38%	0.52%

*Less

Averages

Unsaturated Hydro carbons	0.01%	0.01%	0.01%
Carbon dioxide	0.11%	0.11%	0.12%
Oxygen	18.48%	19.61%	20.38%
Carbon monoxide	0.45%	0.51%	0.45%

Average for West End

Unsaturated Hydro carbons	0.01%
Carbon dioxide	0.11%
Oxygen	19.48%
Carbon monoxide	0.47%

EAST END

	10	11	12	Average
Unsaturated Hydro carbons	*0.01%	0.02%	0.07%	0.03%
Carbon dioxide	0.08%	0.17%	0.19%	0.15%
Oxygen	20.18%	20.03%	20.19%	20.13%
Carbon monoxide	0.35%	0.11%	0.15%	0.20%

	13	14	15	
Unsaturated Hydro carbons	0.02%	0.02%	*0.01%	0.01%
Carbon dioxide	0.07%	0.08%	0.10%	0.08%
Oxygen	19.51%	19.93%	19.50%	19.65%
Carbon monoxide	0.62%	0.52%	0.31%	0.48%

	16	17	18	
Unsaturated Hydro carbons	0.06%	0.06%	0.04%	0.05%
Carbon dioxide	0.21%	0.36%	0.08%	0.22%
Oxygen	20.05%	19.83%	20.38%	20.09%
Carbon monoxide	0.70%	0.35%	0.38%	0.48%

Averages

Unsaturated Hydro carbons	0.03%	0.03%	0.04%
Carbon dioxide	0.12%	0.20%	0.12%
Oxygen	19.91%	19.93%	20.02%
Carbon monoxide	0.06%	0.33....	0.28%

Average for East End

Unsaturated Hydro carbons	0.03%
Carbon dioxide	.15%
Oxygen	19.95%
Carbon monoxide	0.39%

*Less.

Test #3: Date 1/28/17.

Conditions:

All doors closed and ventilators open. Engines of eight cars (arranged as in diagram) all racing for thirty minutes.

WEST END

	1	2	3	Average
Unsaturated Hydro carbons	0.06%	0.07%	0.04%	0.06%
Carbon dioxide	0.14%	0.10%	0.10%	0.11%
Oxygen	20.39%	20.24%	20.21%	20.28%
Carbon monoxide	0.18%	0.12%	0.14%	0.15%

	4	5	6	
Unsaturated Hydro carbons	0.05%	0.04%	0.02%	0.04%
Carbon dioxide	0.18%	0.12%	0.10%	0.13%
Oxygen	20.13%	20.21%	20.37%	20.24%
Carbon monoxide	0.16%	0.23%	0.12%	0.17%

	7	8	9	
Unsaturated Hydro carbons	0.04%	0.02%	0.03%	0.03%
Carbon dioxide	0.15%	0.11%	0.11%	0.12%
Oxygen	20.24%	20.38%	20.40%	20.34%
Carbon monoxide	0.19%	0.25%	0.08%	0.17%

AVERAGES

Unsaturated Hydro carbons	0.05%	0.04%	0.03%
Carbon dioxide	0.16%	0.11%	0.10%
Oxygen	20.25%	20.28%	20.31%
Carbon monoxide	0.18%	0.20%	0.11%

AVERAGE FOR WEST END

Unsaturated Hydro carbons	0.04%
Carbon dioxide	0.12%
Oxygen	20.28%
Carbon monoxide	0.16%

EAST END

	10	11	12	Average
Unsaturated Hydro carbons	0.05%	0.04%	0.08%	0.06%
Carbon dioxide	0.10%	0.11%	0.12%	0.11%
Oxygen	20.49%	20.32%	20.51%	20.44%
Carbon monoxide	0.11%	0.19%	0.18%	0.16%

	13	14	15	
Unsaturated Hydro carbons	0.05%	0.08%	0.15%	0.09%
Carbon dioxide	0.09%	0.11%	0.11%	0.10%
Oxygen	20.50%	20.36%	20.50%	20.45%
Carbon monoxide	0.14%	0.07%	0.21%	0.14%

	16	17	18	
Unsaturated Hydro carbons	0.07%	0.09%	0.12%	0.09%
Carbon dioxide	0.11%	0.11%	0.12%	0.11%
Oxygen	20.35%	20.37%	20.56%	20.43%
Carbon monoxide	0.25%	0.08%	0.07%	0.13%

Averages

Unsaturated Hydro carbons	0.06%	0.07%	0.12%
Carbon dioxide	0.10%	0.11%	0.12%
Oxygen	20.45%	20.33%	20.52%
Carbon monoxide	0.17%	0.11%	0.15%

Average for East End

Unsaturated Hydro carbons	0.08%
Carbon dioxide	0.11%
Oxygen	20.44%
Carbon monoxide	0.14%

Test #4—Date 1/26/17:

Conditions:

All doors closed and ventilators open. Engines of eight cars (arranged as in diagram) all running light for forty minutes.

WEST END

	1	2	3	Average
Unsaturated Hydro carbons	*0.01%	*0.01%	*0.01%	*0.01%
Carbon dioxide	0.02%	0.02%	0.04%	0.03%
Oxygen	20.58%	20.38%	20.66%	20.54%
Carbon monoxide	0.11%	0.09%	0.06%	0.09%

	4	5	6	
Unsaturated Hydro carbons	—	*0.01%	*0.01%	*0.01%
Carbon dioxide	—	0.03%	0.05%	0.04%
Oxygen	—	20.73%	20.55%	20.64%
Carbon monoxide	—	0.09%	0.12%	0.10%

*Less.

	7	8	9	
Unsaturated Hydro carbons	*0.01%	*0.01%	*0.01%	*0.01%
Carbon dioxide	0.06%	0.03%	0.06%	0.05%
Oxygen	20.31%	20.50%	20.95%	20.58%
Carbon monoxide	0.09%	0.06%	0.02%	0.06%

AVERAGES

Unsaturated Hydro carbons	*0.01%	*0.01%	*0.01%
Carbon dioxide	0.04%	0.03%	0.05%
Oxygen	20.45%	20.54%	20.72%
Carbon monoxide	0.10%	0.08%	0.07%

AVERAGE FOR WEST END

Unsaturated Hydro carbons	Less than 0.01%
Carbon dioxide	0.04%
Oxygen	20.57%
Carbon monoxide	0.08%

EAST END

	10	11	12	Average
Unsaturated Hydro carbons	*0.01%	*0.01%	*0.01%	*0.01%
Carbon dioxide	0.04%	0.04%	0.04%	0.04%
Oxygen	20.51%	20.73%	20.34%	20.53%
Carbon monoxide	0.08%	0.02%	0.10%	0.07%

	13	14	15	
Unsaturated Hydro carbons	*0.01%	*0.01%	*0.01%	*0.01%
Carbon dioxide	0.04%	0.06%	0.05%	0.05%
Oxygen	20.61%	20.76%	20.61%	20.66%
Carbon monoxide	0.08%	0.07%	0.09%	0.08%

	16	17	18	
Unsaturated Hydro carbons	*0.01%	*0.01%	*0.01%	*0.01%
Carbon dioxide	0.10%	0.11%	0.12%	0.11%
Oxygen	20.60%	20.16%	20.28%	20.34%
Carbon monoxide	0.05%	0.03%	0.12%	0.07%

AVERAGES

Unsaturated Hydro carbons	*0.01%	*0.01%	*0.01%
Carbon dioxide	0.07%	0.07%	0.07%
Oxygen	20.57%	20.55%	20.41%
Carbon monoxide	0.07%	0.04%	0.10%

AVERAGE FOR EAST END

Unsaturated Hydro carbons	Less than 0.01%
Carbon dioxide	0.07%
Oxygen	20.51%
Carbon monoxide	0.07%

* Less.

Test #5—Date 1/30/17:

Conditions:

Same as in Test #3, except that the direction of ventilation was reversed, the air entering the experimental tunnel at the top and leaving by the side ventilators on the floor.

WEST END

	1	2	3	Average
Unsaturated Hydro carbons	0.06%	0.04%	0.06%	0.05%
Carbon dioxide	0.07%	0.06%	0.07%	0.07%
Oxygen	20.36%	20.58%	20.58%	20.51%
Carbon monoxide	0.31%	0.11%	0.09%	0.17%

	4	5	6	
Unsaturated Hydro carbons	0.05%	0.06%	0.07%	0.06%
Carbon dioxide	0.07%	0.08%	0.08%	0.08%
Oxygen	20.48%	20.43%	20.51%	20.47%
Carbon monoxide	0.12%	0.21%	0.17%	0.17%

	7	8	9	
Unsaturated Hydro carbons	0.08%	0.11%	0.08%	0.09%
Carbon dioxide	0.09%	0.08%	0.07%	0.08%
Oxygen	20.43%	20.27%	20.45%	20.38%
Carbon monoxide	0.19%	0.11%	0.19%	0.16%

Averages

Unsaturated Hydro carbons	0.06%	0.07%	0.07%
Carbon dioxide	0.08%	0.07%	0.07%
Oxygen	20.42%	20.43%	20.51%
Carbon monoxide	0.21%	0.14%	0.15%

Average for West End

Unsaturated Hydro carbons	0.07%
Carbon dioxide	0.07%
Oxygen	20.45%
Carbon monoxide	0.17%

EAST END

	10	11	12	Average
Unsaturated Hydro carbons	0.09%	0.05%	0.05%	0.06%
Carbon dioxide	0.14%	0.20%	0.18%	0.17%
Oxygen	20.58%	20.59%	20.54%	20.57%
Carbon monoxide	0.31%	0.33%	0.18%	0.27%

	13	14	15	
Unsaturated Hydro carbons	0.12%	0.10%	0.08%	0.10%
Carbon dioxide	0.14%	0.15%	0.14%	0.14%
Oxygen	20.43%	20.43%	20.51%	20.46%
Carbon monoxide	0.23%	0.22%	0.16%	0.20%
	16	17	18	
Unsaturated Hydro carbons	0.13%	0.13%	0.13%	0.13%
Carbon dioxide	0.14%	0.13%	0.18%	0.15%
Oxygen	20.51%	20.38%	20.52%	20.47%
Carbon monoxide	0.12%	0.43%	0.39%	0.31%

Averages

Unsaturated Hydro carbons	0.11%	0.09%	0.09%
Carbon dioxide	0.14%	0.16%	0.17%
Oxygen	20.51%	20.47%	20.52%
Carbon monoxide	0.22%	0.33%	0.24%

Average for East End

Unsaturated Hydro carbons	0.10%
Carbon dioxide	0.16%
Oxygen	20.50%
Carbon monoxide	0.26%

Test #6—Date 2/1/17.

Conditions:

Same as in Test #4, except that the direction of ventilation was reversed, the air entering the experimental tunnel at the top and leaving by the side ventilators on the floor.

WEST END

	1	2	3	Average
Unsaturated Hydro carbons	0.02%	0.01%	0.02%	0.02%
Carbon dioxide	0.07%	0.09%	0.07%	0.08%
Oxygen	20.54%	20.49%	20.53%	20.52%
Carbon monoxide	0.11%	0.22%	0.17%	0.17%
	4	5	6	
Unsaturated Hydro carbons	0.01%	0.03%	0.04%	0.03%
Carbon dioxide	0.07%	0.08%	0.05%	0.07%
Oxygen	20.64%	20.55%	20.38%	20.48%
Carbon monoxide	0.13%	0.24%	0.09%	0.15%

	7	8	9	
Unsaturated Hydro carbons	0.05%	0.06%	0.06%	0.06%
Carbon dioxide	0.10%	0.11%	0.09%	0.10%
Oxygen	20.42%	20.51%	20.37%	20.43%
Carbon monoxide	0.22%	0.09%	0.38%	0.23%

Averages

Unsaturated Hydro carbons	0.03%	0.03%	0.04%
Carbon dioxide	0.08%	0.09%	0.07%
Oxygen	20.53%	20.52%	20.46%
Carbon monoxide	0.15%	0.18%	0.21%

Average for West End

Unsaturated Hydro carbons	0.03%
Carbon dioxide	0.08%
Oxygen	20.50%
Carbon monoxide	0.18%

EAST END

	10	11	12	Average
Unsaturated Hydro carbons	0.06%	0.06%	0.05%	0.06%
Carbon dioxide	0.07%	0.08%	0.09%	0.08%
Oxygen	20.61%	20.53%	20.63%	20.59%
Carbon monoxide	0.10%	0.26%	0.11%	0.16%

	13	14	15	
Unsaturated Hydro carbons	0.11%	0.07%	0.06%	0.08%
Carbon dioxide	0.09%	0.10%	0.10%	0.10%
Oxygen	20.58%	20.55%	20.59%	20.57%
Carbon monoxide	0.11%	0.16%	0.18%	0.15%

	16	17	18	
Unsaturated Hydro carbons	0.07%	0.04%	0.09%	0.07%
Carbon dioxide	0.10%	0.10%	0.13%	0.11%
Oxygen	20.59%	20.41%	20.61%	20.54%
Carbon monoxide	0.31%	0.32%	0.31%	0.31%

Averages

Unsaturated Hydro carbons	0.08%	0.06%	0.07%
Carbon dioxide	0.09%	0.09%	0.11%
Oxygen	20.59%	20.50%	20.61%
Carbon monoxide	0.17%	0.25%	0.20%

Average for East End

Unsaturated Hydro carbons	0.07%
Carbon dioxide	0.10%
Oxygen	20.57%
Carbon monoxide	0.21%

AVERAGE RESULTS OF AIR ANALYSES IN EXPERIMENTAL TUNNEL

Test #1:	East End	West End	Whole Tunnel
Unsaturated Hydro carbons	0.15%	0.34%	0.25%
Carbon dioxide	0.42%	0.60%	0.51%
Oxygen	19.22%	18.90%	19.06%
Carbon monoxide	0.59%	0.57%	0.58%

Test #2:			
Unsaturated Hydro carbons	0.03%	0.01%	0.02%
Carbon dioxide	0.15%	0.11%	0.13%
Oxygen	19.95%	19.48%	19.72%
Carbon monoxide	0.39%	0.47%	0.43%

Test #3:			
Unsaturated Hydro carbons	0.08%	0.04%	0.06%
Carbon dioxide	0.11%	0.12%	0.12%
Oxygen	20.44%	20.28%	20.36%
Carbon monoxide	0.14%	0.16%	0.15%

Test #4:			
Unsaturated Hydro carbons	*0.01%	*0.01%	*0.01%
Carbon dioxide	0.07%	0.04%	0.06%
Oxygen	20.51%	20.57%	20.54%
Carbon monoxide	0.07%	0.08%	0.075%

Test #5:			
Unsaturated Hydro carbons	0.10%	0.07%	0.09%
Carbon dioxide	0.16%	0.07%	0.12%
Oxygen	20.50%	20.45%	20.48%
Carbon monoxide	0.26%	0.17%	0.22%

Test #6:			
Unsaturated Hydro carbons	0.07%	0.03%	0.05%
Carbon dioxide	0.10%	0.08%	0.09%
Oxygen	20.57%	20.50%	20.54%
Carbon monoxide	0.21%	0.18%	0.20%

* Less.

CONCLUSIONS

From the analytical results obtained the following conclusions are drawn:

1. When all doors and ventilators are closed and the engines of eight cars (arranged as in diagram) are racing for thirty minutes, the atmosphere becomes intolerable; the high content of unsaturated hydro carbons ("smoke") being responsible for a marked irritation of the eyes and respiratory organs, and the carbon monoxide producing distressing physiological disturbances. Such an atmosphere must be regarded as dangerous to persons who breathe it for a continuous period of fifteen minutes.

2. When all doors and ventilators are closed and the engines of eight cars (arranged as in diagram) are "running light" for thirty minutes, there is a marked improvement in the condition of the atmosphere as indicated under Test 2, but the breathing of such an atmosphere for a continuous period of fifteen minutes must also be regarded as dangerous.

3. When all doors are closed and the ventilators are open and exhausting from the top of the tunnel, with the engines of eight cars (arranged as in diagram) racing for thirty minutes, there is a further improvement in the condition of the atmosphere over that indicated under Test 1 and Test 2. However, the carbon monoxide content of this atmosphere must be looked upon as probably dangerous either to those persons who are physiologically weak, or to those persons who are particularly susceptible to this gas and who breathe it for a continuous period of thirty minutes.

4. When all doors are closed and the ventilators are open and exhausting from the top of the tunnel, with the engines of eight cars (arranged as in diagram) "running light" for forty minutes, the condition of the atmosphere is almost normal and the carbon monoxide content is not dangerous.

This conclusion is further supported by the fact that the eighteen persons who remained in the tunnel during this test, for a continuous period of forty minutes, experienced no unpleasant sensations from breathing this air and no subsequent distress.

5. When all doors are closed and the ventilators are open and exhausting from the bottom of the tunnel, with the engines of eight cars (arranged as in diagram) all racing for thirty minutes, the condition of the atmosphere is much worse than in Test 3, where the same conditions prevailed, except that the exhaust was made from the top of the tunnel. Such an atmosphere is not only unpleasant, but must be regarded as dangerous if breathed continuously for a period of thirty minutes.

6. When all doors are closed and the ventilators are open and exhausting from the bottom of the tunnel, with the engines of eight cars (arranged as in diagram) all running light for thirty minutes, there is only a slight improvement in the condition of the atmosphere over that indicated in Test 5. Moreover, the condition of this atmosphere is much worse than the air in Test 4, when the same conditions prevailed, except that the exhaust was made from the

top of the tunnel. Such an atmosphere is unpleasant and must be regarded as dangerous if breathed continuously for a period of thirty minutes.

7. It appears that the direction of the exhaust air is of considerable importance, the most satisfactory results being obtained when the air enters the tunnel at the bottom and is withdrawn at the top. This was to be expected because of the fact that the exhaust gases leave the motors at a high temperature and are consequently lighter than air, and rapidly diffuse upward. The lateral propulsion of these heated exhaust gases into the atmosphere produces a motion which mixes the exhaust gases with the air, thus accounting for the fairly uniform distribution of the products of combustion in the atmosphere of the various parts of the tunnel.

8. Some of the odors which are unpleasant are in no sense dangerous and are produced by the "cracking" of lubricating oil.

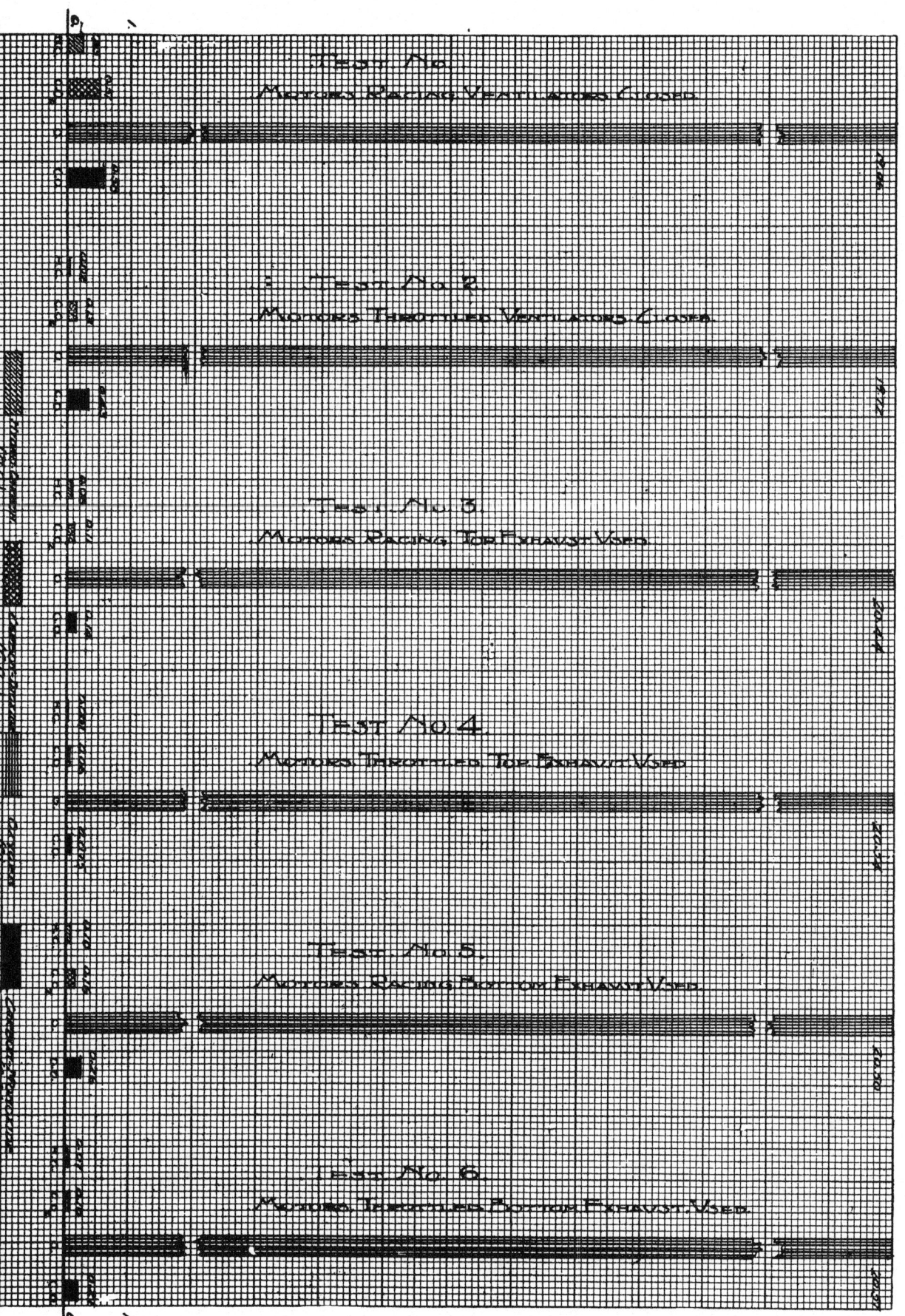

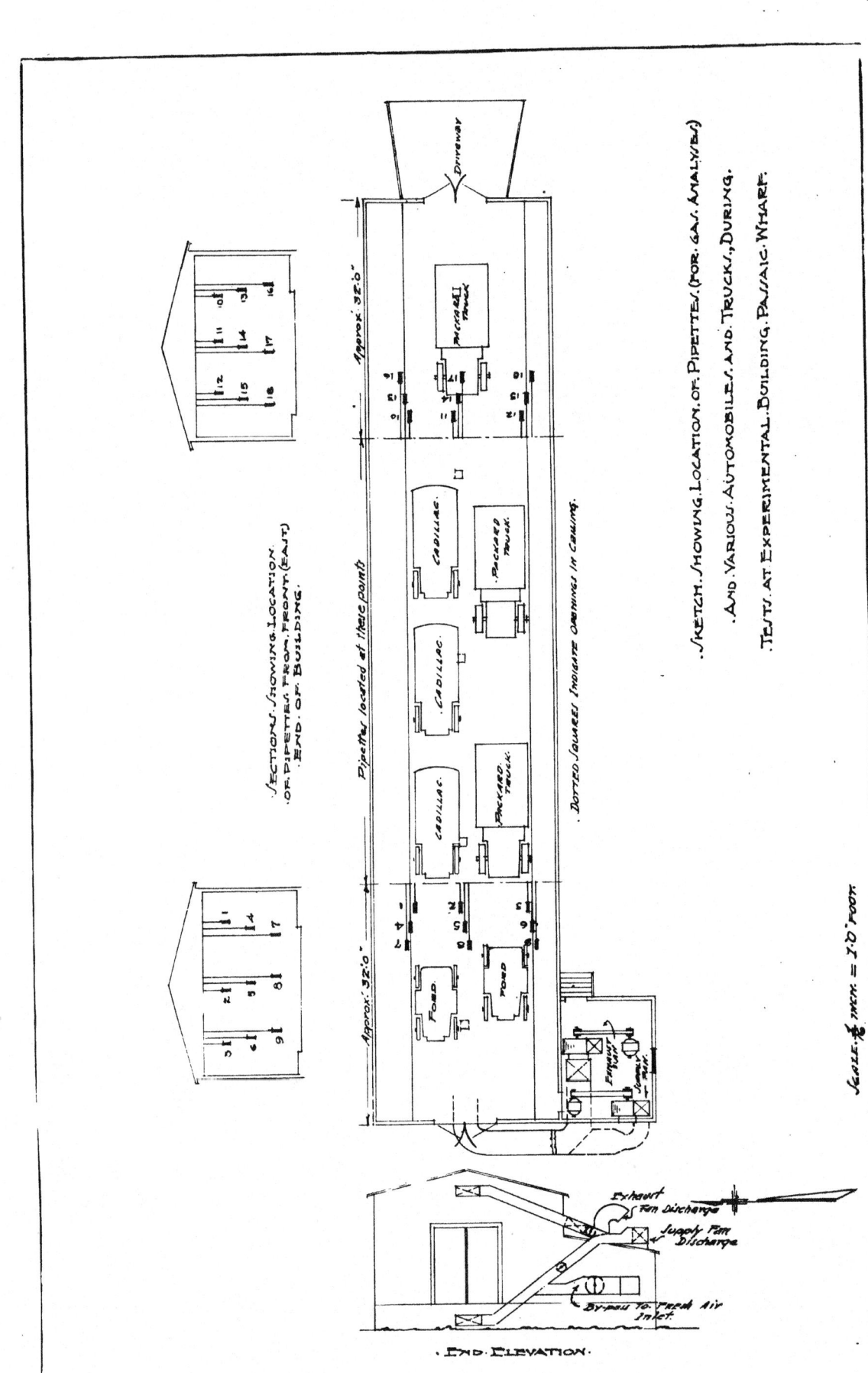

APPENDIX No. 11.

REAL ESTATE.

The Board has in its report intentionally refrained from any general discussion of the real estate question. The plans show the use of private property for the Jersey City terminus. The Board anticipates that the construction of the tunnel will increase the value of properties adjacent to its Jersey City terminus for use as sites for storage warehouses, small factory lofts and similar buildings. If the tunnel were on private property it would not prevent the use of that property as a site for a building, as it will require only part of the cellar and part of the ground floor for tunnel passageways through a building entirely covering the site.

On the New York side the plans show the use of a portion of Canal Street as the terminus. It is improbable that the City authorities would permit such use unless arrangements were made to considerably increase the width of Canal Street, where the outlet of the tunnel encroaches on the surface of the street. Such widening could be made only by the condemnation and purchase of a strip of private property along one or both sides of the street. It would probably be cheaper to condemn the entire properties on one side of the street and dispose of remnants not required for the widening, or to purchase an entire block north or south of the terminal opening and later utilize the plot as the site of a building. Your Board is of the opinion that property purchased at a reasonable price suited to the location might yield a satisfactory return on the investment. The cost of the building would not be greatly increased by the necessity of spanning the tunnel passages, nor would its use for storage purposes be interfered with beyond the loss to the building of the spaces used by the tunnel.

The Board has considered Spring Street as a location for the New York approach. This location would avoid the large sewer on Canal Street, and if suitable property could be purchased for the above described purposes at a reasonable price, this location might be cheaper and, all things considered, better than the Canal Street location.

The use of West Street would avoid the necessity of purchasing any New York real estate. The Board has made no inquiry as to the feasibility of securing from the City permission to use West Street, nor as to the rentals or payments, if any, which the City would require for such use.

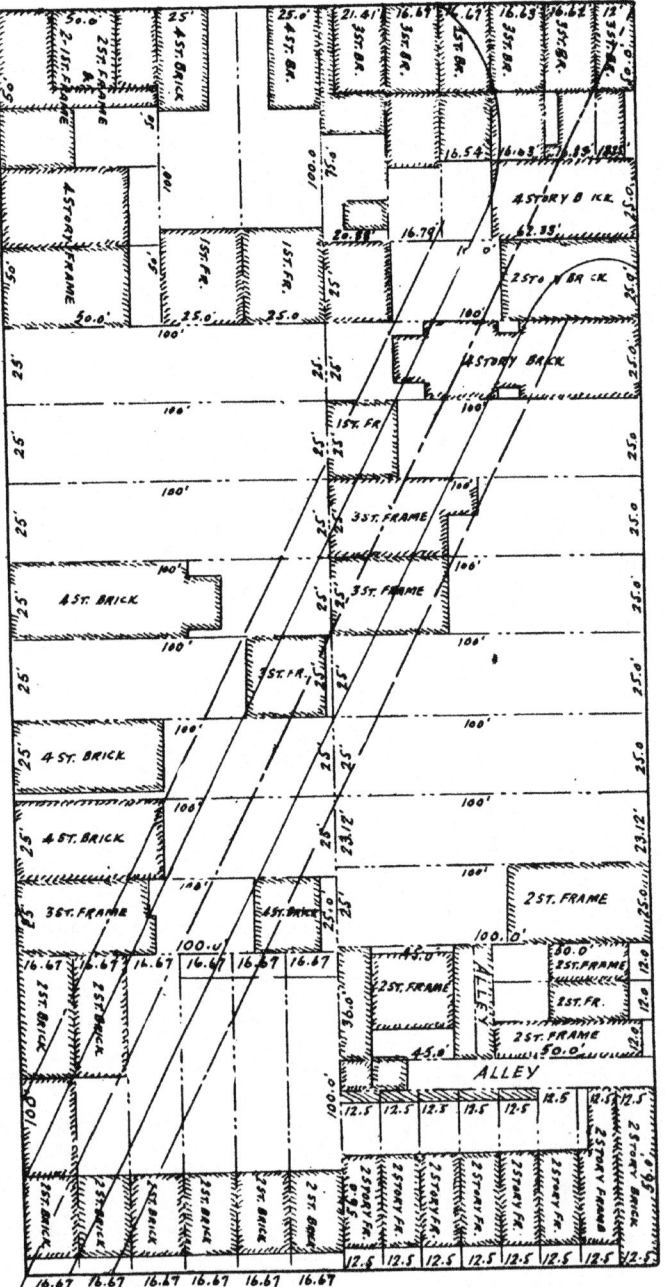

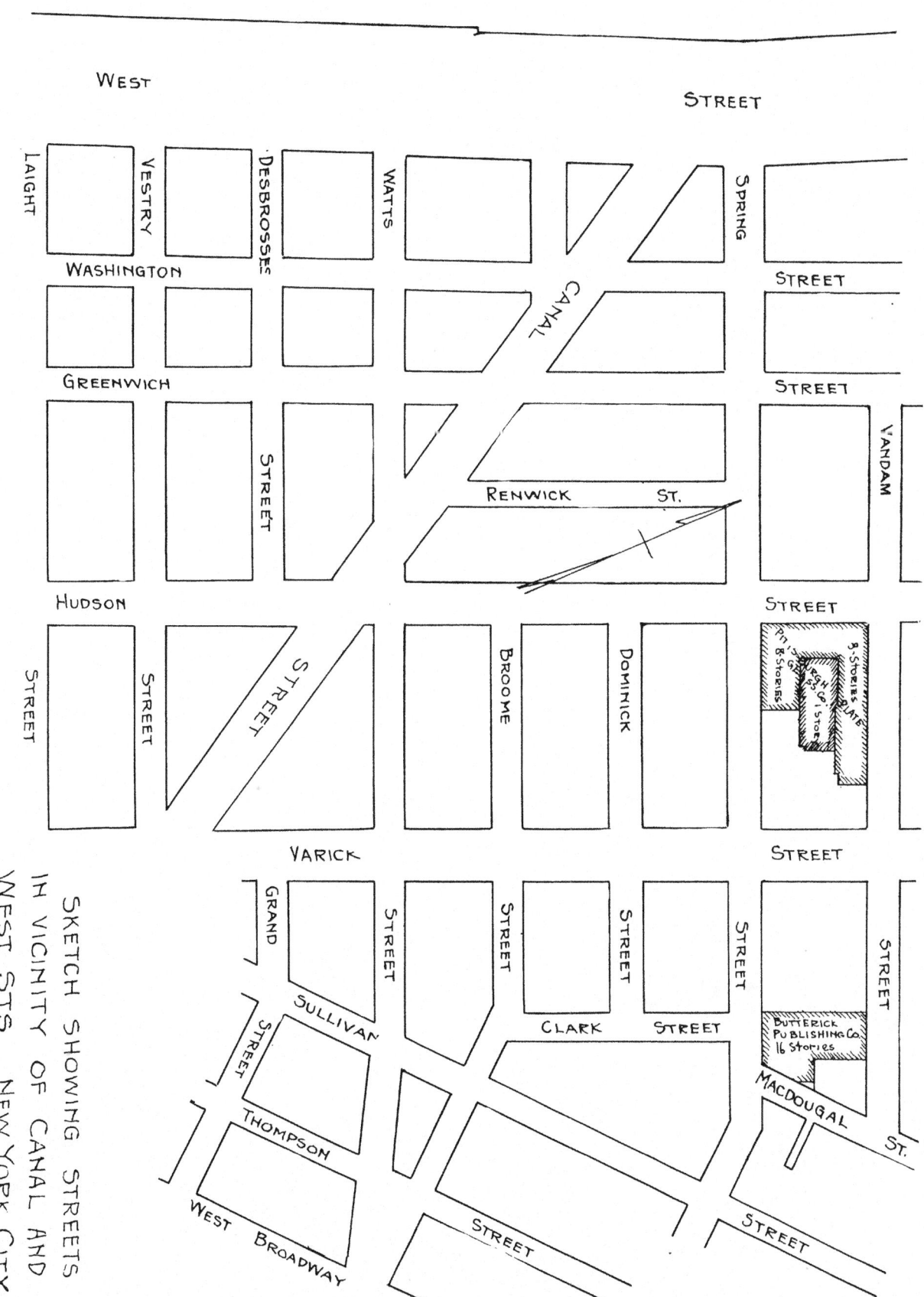

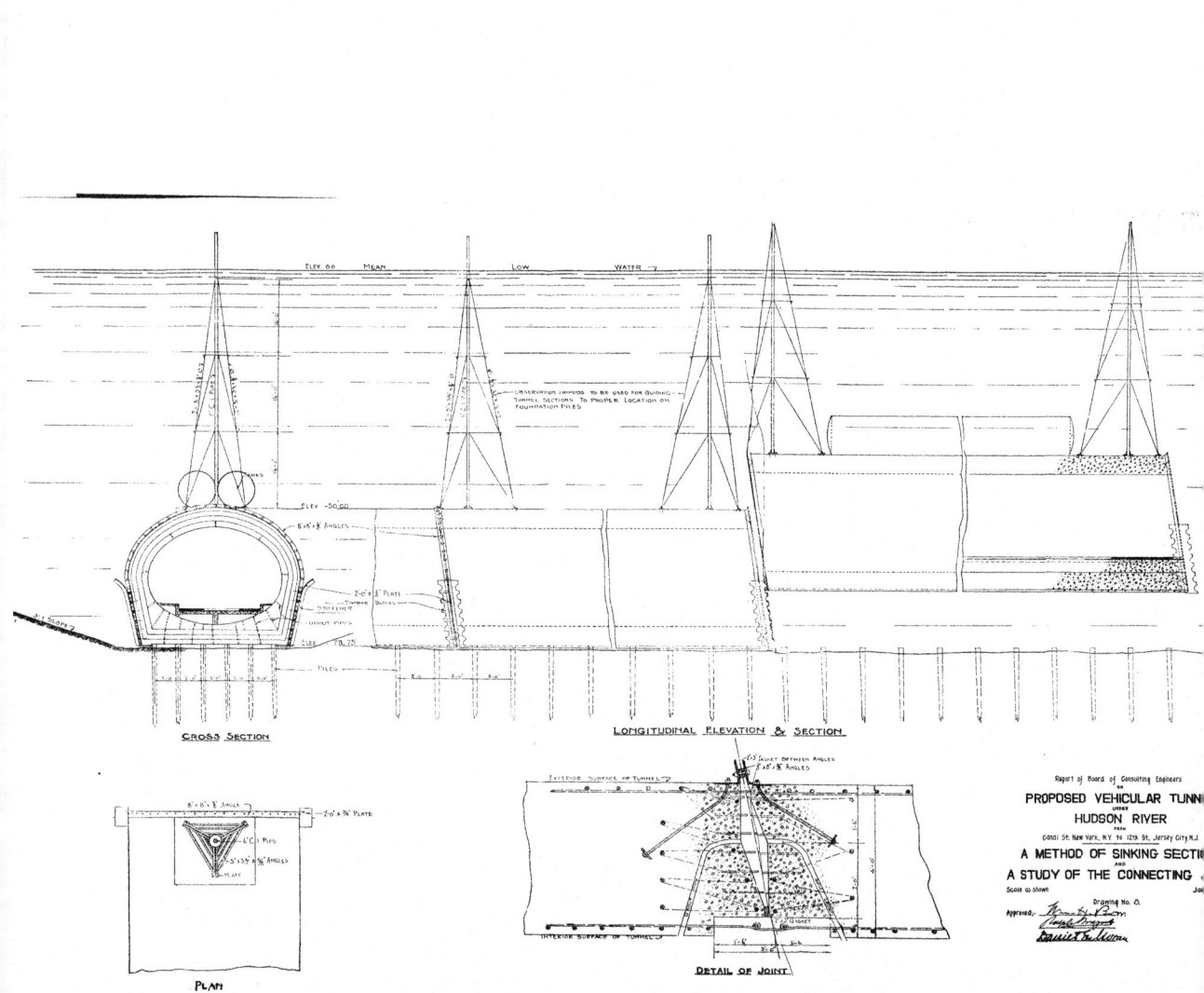

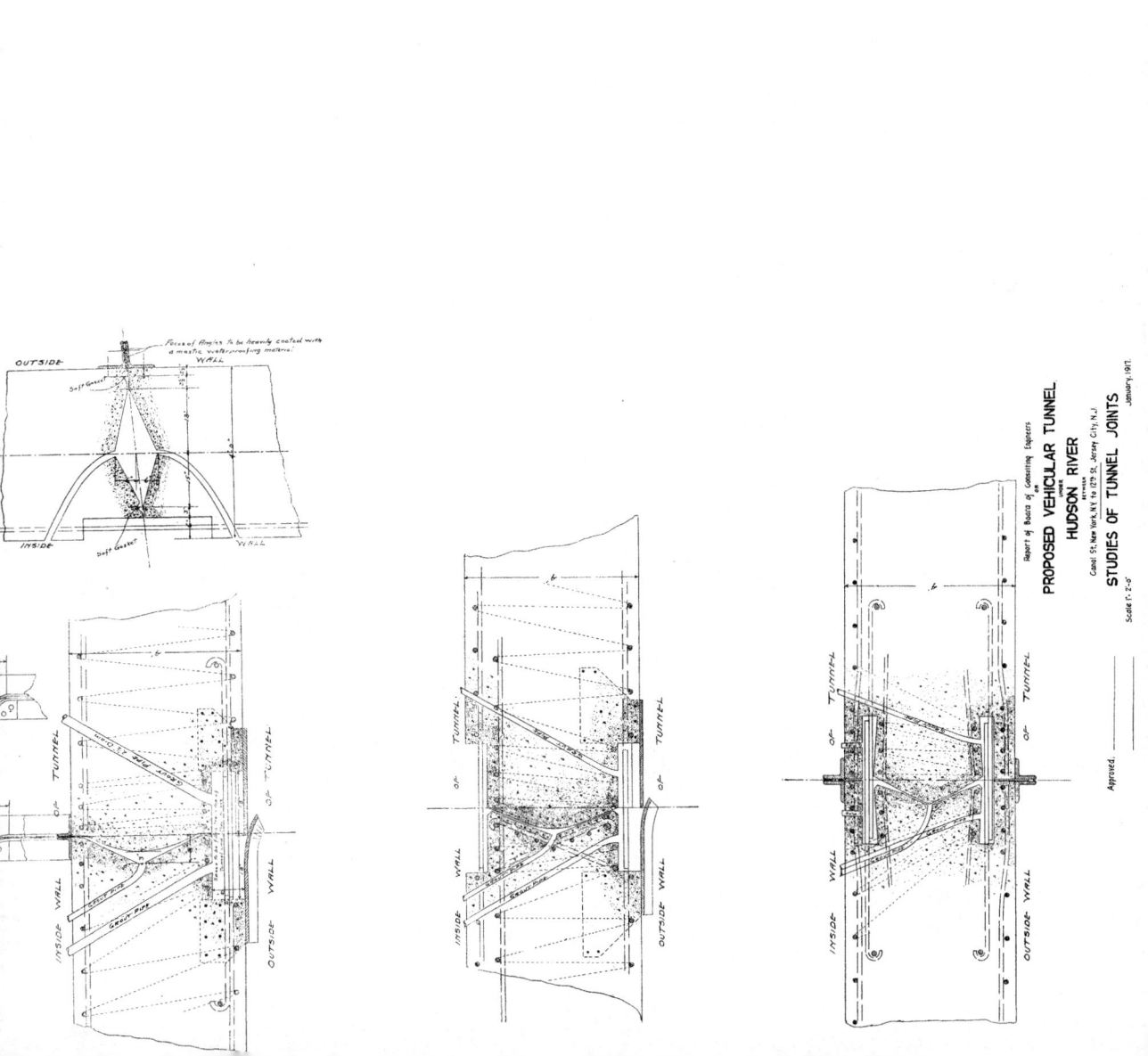

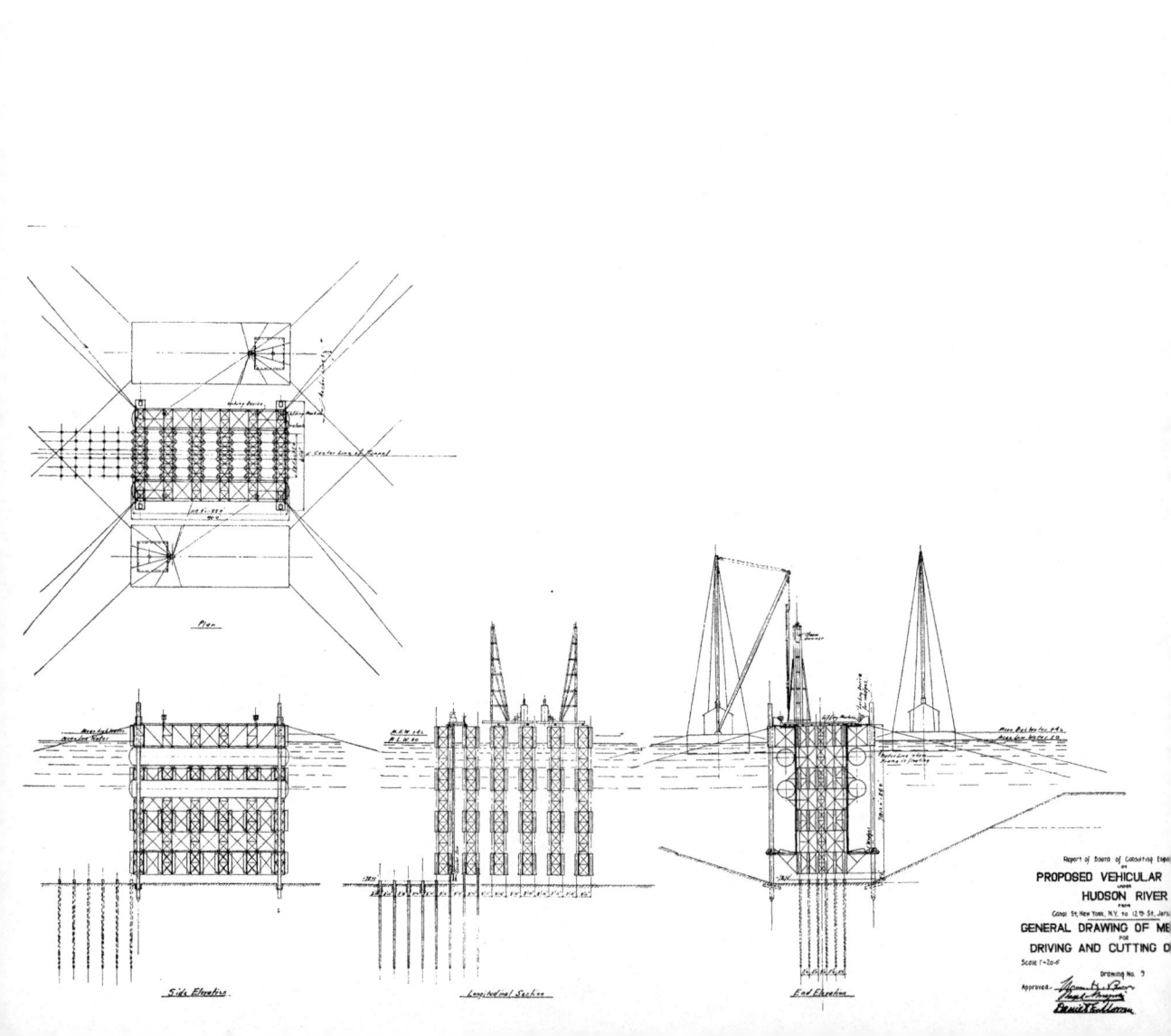

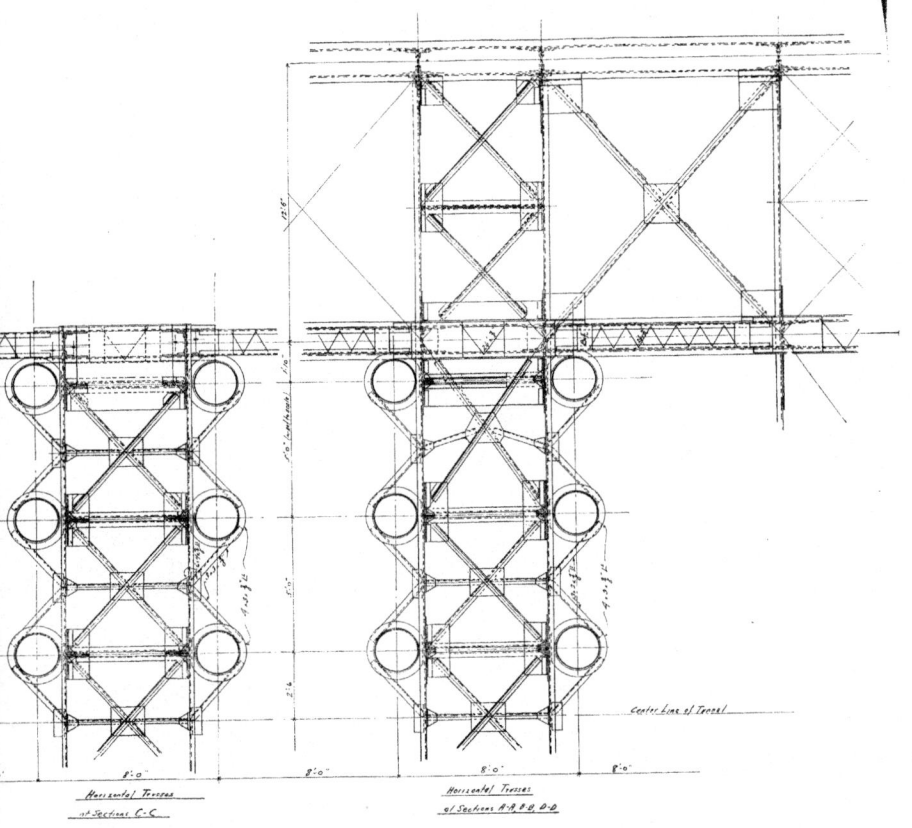

Oversized Foldout

Oversized Foldout

Oversized Foldout

Oversized Foldout

Oversized Foldout

EXHIBIT 8.

TABLE SHOWING CAPACITY OF TUNNEL

TABLE SHOWING HOURLY WEEK DAY USE OF TUNNEL BASED ON 2,000,000 VEHICLES PASSING THROUGH PER YEAR

Length of covered tunnel, 9409.19′. Speed, 10 miles per hour. Time required for vehicle to pass through tunnel, 10.7 minutes

HOUR	Estimated No. of vehicles using Cortlandt, Barclay, Chambers, Desbrosses and Christopher Street Ferries in 1920, by hours.	No. of vehicles estimated as motor driven and which are assumed as diverted to tunnel, being 50% of previous column (both ways), by hours.	Assuming traffic in 1920 as equally divided going to and coming from New York. No. of vehicles using tunnel one way, by hours.	Average distance vehicles would be apart.	No. of vehicles both ways in the tunnel at one time.
A. M.					
12 to 1	224	112	56	1029	20
1 to 2	243	122	61	925	22
2 to 3	221	111	55	1029	20
3 to 4	250	125	63	880	23
4 to 5	291	146	73	768	26
5 to 6	338	169	85	633	31
6 to 7	525	263	131	412	47
7 to 8	867	434	217	233	78
8 to 9	1054	527	264	189	94
9 to 10	1022	511	256	192	92
10 to 11	957	479	239	209	86
11 to 12	861	431	215	217	83
P. M.					
12 to 1	702	351	176	293	63
1 to 2	765	383	191	266	69
2 to 3	872	436	218	233	78
3 to 4	812	406	203	250	73
4 to 5	764	382	191	266	69
5 to 6	832	416	208	242	75
6 to 7	719	360	180	284	65
7 to 8	408	204	102	522	37
8 to 9	255	128	64	880	23
9 to 10	272	136	68	802	25
10 to 11	197	99	49	1160	18
11 to 12	228	114	57	974	21

Date Due

TF
238
.H73
P98

Public service cor-
poration of New
Jersey
Report

GROEBE-McGOVERN COMPANY
PRINTERS
NEWARK, N. J.

Printed in Dunstable, United Kingdom